The
Thoughts of José Valdez IV

As told to Clint Crockett

The Thoughts of José Valdez IV

As told to Clint Crockett

iUniverse, Inc.

New York   Bloomington

iUniverse books may be ordered through booksellers or by contacting:

iUniverse
1663 Liberty Drive
Bloomington, IN 47403
www.iuniverse.com
1-800-Authors (1-800-288-4677)

Because of the dynamic nature of the Internet, any Web addresses or links contained in this book may have changed since publication and may no longer be valid. The views expressed in this work are solely those of the author and do not necessarily reflect the views of the publisher, and the publisher hereby disclaims any responsibility for them.

ISBN: 978-1-4401-5734-9 (sc)
ISBN: 978-1-4401-5735-6 (ebook)

Printed in the United States of America

iUniverse rev. date: 8/26/2009

For Janna, the Wife Whose Name Shall be Spoken.

Introduction

José Valdez IV is a thrice married, tequila drinking, conflicted Presbyterian with a (minor) criminal record. He is infatuated with Salma Hayek, has had numerous Bigfoot sightings, and is somewhat of a stalker of Ole Miss coaches. In other words, he's just like any other guy.

I have probably never been more dejected as an Ole Miss fan than I was after the 2007 Egg Bowl, a particularly devastating loss. Shortly after the game I went online to the Ole Miss Spirit message board. It was in full meltdown mode. While I shared most of the emotions being exhibited by the posters, it made me realize how out of balance my priorities were. Losing a football game (albeit the most important one of the Ole Miss season) should not have the kind of impact it was having on so many of the fans, myself included. I decided I would try to add some levity to the situation.

As a huge Boston Red Sox fan, I had discovered *José Melendez's Keys to the Game*, a few months prior. *Keys to the Game* is an amazing blog, written in third person, which touches on almost any subject you can conceive. After giving it some thought, I decided I would post something on the Ole Miss Spirit message board in a similar style. I wish I had come up with this idea on my own, but I am not that original a thinker.

The day following the Egg Bowl loss, I posted "The Thoughts of Jose Valdez IV". The reaction to my post was not overwhelming, but it was favorable. What encouraged me was that one of the responses came from a friend of mine and huge Rebel fan, Jody Varner, who had no idea I was the one who had written the thoughts. I decided at that point to continue posting as José Valdez IV for the time being.

Even though his writings were on the Red Sox and mine were on Ole Miss, it was important to me that I differentiate my work from that of José

Melendez in another way. I chose to do this by making José Valdez IV a character, giving him a personal history and recording his misadventures. As the thoughts evolved, I added additional characters such as Jorge and Paco, The Wife Whose Name Shall Not be Spoken, Jose III, and others. José Melendez doesn't write this way, probably because he doesn't have to. His material is brilliant just the way it is. Unfortunately, one of the drawbacks of writing the José Valdez IV material is that I no longer read *Keys to the Game* because I do not want to be guilty of using the same references that he does.

Shortly after my initial thoughts, Ed Orgeron was relieved of his duties as the Ole Miss football coach and names of potential candidates for the position began to surface. I wrote an essay "José's Thoughts on the Candidates" which received many favorable responses and it just took on a life of its own after that.

After posting José's thoughts only on the Ole Miss Spirit board for a couple of months, I began posting them on the RebelSports.net site as well and have been very pleased with the reception from Ole Miss fans there. The thoughts have also been received graciously by many Wake Forest fans after my selection about their school this past football season. I am especially pleased that some of them have declared that they now root for Ole Miss when the Deacons are not their opponent.

The thoughts of José Valdez IV included in this book are in the exact order in which they were written and have not been changed, other than to correct any typos or punctuation mistakes. If there are grammatical errors, well that's just the way José thought them. For those who may be interested, I have added a section of notes at the end of each thought which offers some background information.

Writing these thoughts and reading the responses to them has made the last year and a half an extremely enjoyable time for me as an Ole Miss fan. I appreciate all of the comments and hope to continue writing as long as I am able and as long as ridiculous ideas keep popping up in my head.

Clint Crockett
May, 2009

Table of Contents

Introduction   iii

José Valdez IV's Thoughts   1

José's Thoughts on the Candidates   3

José's Thoughts on Coach Nutt   6

José's Thoughts on Troy   8

Jose's Random Thoughts   10

José's Thoughts on New Mexico   12

José's Thoughts on Central Florida   15

José's Thoughts on His Best Ole Miss Experience   17

José's Thoughts on His Worst Ole Miss Sports Experience   19

José's Thoughts on Ole Miss Basketball   21

José's Thoughts on Winthrop   24

José's Thoughts on DePaul   27

José's Thoughts on La Salle   30

José's Thoughts on Clemson   33

José's Thoughts on The Eagles   36

José's Thoughts on 2007   39

José's Thoughts on Alabama A&M   42

José's Thoughts on Tennessee   45

José's Thoughts on LSU with Special Commentary from José III   48

José's Thoughts on Florida   51

José's Thoughts on Auburn   55

José's Thoughts on the School Whose Name Shall Not be Spoken   58

José's Thoughts on the Super Bowl   61

José's Thoughts on Vanderbilt   64

José's Thoughts on South Carolina   67

José's Thoughts on Arkansas   70

José's Thoughts on Presbyterian   73

José's Thoughts on Alabama   76

José's Thoughts on Auburn Chapter Dos   79

José's Thoughts on The School Whose Name Shall Not be Spoken Chapter Dos   82

José's Thoughts on Minnesota   85

José's Thoughts on LSU Chapter Dos   89

José's Thoughts on Northwestern State   90

José's Thoughts on Kentucky   93

José's Thoughts on Indiana State   96

José's Thoughts on Alabama Chapter Dos   98

José's Thoughts on the NIT   100

José's Thoughts on the NIT Final Four   103

José's Thoughts on the Ole Miss Baseball Season Thus Far   106

José's Thoughts   108

José's Thoughts   111

José's Thoughts   113

José's Thoughts on the Letter   116

José's Thoughts on the 1977 Notre Dame Game   119

José's Thoughts on the Powe Situation   122

José's Thoughts on the 1983 Egg Bowl   125

José's Thoughts on the Summer   129

José's Thoughts on Powe Gaining His Eligibility   131

José's Preseason 2008 Football Thoughts   133

José's Thoughts on Memphis State   135

José's Thoughts on Wake Forest   138

Jose Valdez III's Thoughts on Nutt's First Game   141

José's Thoughts on Stanford   143

José's Thoughts on Vanderbilt Chapter Dos   146

José's Thoughts on Florida Chapter Dos   149

José's Thoughts on South Carolina Chapter Dos   152

José's Thoughts on Alabama Chapter Tres   155

José's Thoughts on Arkansas Chapter Dos   158

José's Thoughts on Auburn Chapter Tres   162

José's Thoughts on Louisiana-Monroe   166

José's Thoughts on LSU Chapter Tres   170

José's Thoughts on The School Whose Name Shall Not be Spoken Chapter Tres   174

Jose's Thoughts on the Egg Bowl   177

José's Thoughts on Madrid   180

José's Thoughts on the Kennedy Situation   182

José's Thoughts on Texas Tech   185

José's Thoughts on the Cotton Bowl   189

José's Thoughts   192

José's (Painfully Long) Thoughts on the 2009 Recruiting Class Part One
195

José's Thoughts on the 2009 Recruiting Class Part Dos   202

José's Thoughts on the 2009 Recruiting Class Part Tres   208

José's Thoughts on the 12th Opponent   214

José's thoughts on The School Whose Name Shall Not be Spoken Chapter Cuatro   217

José's Thoughts on Double Decker Weekend   219

José's Thoughts on The School Whose Name Shall Not be Spoken Chapter Cinco   222

José's Thoughts on the SEC Championship   225

José's Thoughts on Virginia   228

Acknowledgements   231

José Valdez IV's Thoughts

The past few days have been difficult for José. He watched his Rebels surrender a 14-0 lead to the team whose name shall not be spoken in less time than it takes José to run 1600 meters (Just as Justin Timberlake is bringing sexy back, José is attempting to bring the metric system back). José had been on the fence about the Rebel coach before this game, not sure if he was the right man for the job, but fully believing he deserved another year to have the opportunity to, how you say?, "right the ship". José even got into heated discussions with his father, José III, about the Rebel coach. (José III is one of those Ole Miss graduates who went to school during the Vaught years and constantly reminds you how many games they lost while he was in school. You know the type). After the game against the team whose name shall not be spoken, José came to the realization that this metaphorical ship was sinking, could not be righted, and must be abandoned or risk the peril of an agonizing death. *Note: José saw Titanic and is fully cognizant that abandoning ship doesn't always work out either.*

What José has missed most recently has been the excitement of waking up on a Saturday morning and knowing that his team was going to play a football game that had bowl game implications. José doesn't like playing games that determine whether or not his team finishes in 5th or 6th place in the SEC West (until the SEC West expands to 30 or 40 teams, 5th or 6th will not be that good), or whether they finish with a single win. He also doesn't like going to games where the crowd is so small that he is able to strike up conversations with each and every fan in the stadium. (Although José certainly enjoyed meeting Mrs. Grace Tuttle from Winona and sincerely hopes that her "situation" with the yard man has been resolved amicably). Put simply, José has had the joy of being an Ole Miss football fan sucked from his very being.

The situation is not much unlike that with José's 3rd wife, or the wife whose name shall not be spoken. He had some good years with wife #2, one year was particularly good, but the last year was very bad. José probably should have played the field a little more before marrying the wife whose name shall not be spoken, but she was very convincing, the wine was sweet, and she most assuredly wanted to be married. Many of José's friends predicted things would end badly, but did José listen? No he did not. Perhaps José gave up on the marriage too early, but he could not continue in the marriage with things the way they were. José is excited that he has some prospects for wife #4 and will let you know how that turns out.

My name is José Valdez IV, and these are my thoughts.

Notes:

- **I covered my reasons for writing these thoughts in the Introduction. It was an extremely depressing time to be an Ole Miss fan and I felt a little better after writing this.**

- **In these original thoughts I referred to them (I still won't write the name) as "the team whose name shall not be spoken". In subsequent thoughts they became "The School Whose Name Shall Not be Spoken" or TSWNSNBS.**

José's Thoughts on the Candidates

José has given much consideration to the pool of potential head coaching candidates and would like to share his thoughts on a few of them.

Rick Neuheisel- Because this coach's last name is very similar to his favorite beer, Newcastle, José is fine with this candidate. José knows what you are thinking, "With a name like José Valdez IV, shouldn't your favorite beer be something like Corona or Dos XX's and not an English one?" José pities you for falling into the trap of stereotyping people in such a way.

Dennis Franchione- José cannot support this candidate. After all what kind of name is Franchione? Is it French or Italian? No matter, because José does not like any French or Italians. The name Franchione also reminds José of Generalissimo Francisco Franco, who he despised. Again, he knows what you are thinking. "But José, wasn't the Fascist Franco the lesser of two evils in the Spanish Civil War? Are you a Communist sympathizer?" José is not a communist sympathizer, but he understands where you are coming from. The atrocities committed by Franco and his group far outweighed those of the Spanish Loyalists and with this in mind José cannot support Generalissimo Dennis Franchione.

Gary Patterson- José hears that Patterson is a cat person. José is a dog person.

Skip Holtz- Because José is a dog person one would think that he would throw his full support behind a coach who was named after Willie Morris' dog. José would prefer that if the Rebel coach were named after one of

Willie's dogs, it be after his black lab Pete, but José is not confident in the prospects of convincing the USC coach named Pete to come to Oxford.

Dan Mullen- Mullen is at Florida. José has been to Florida and likes it. He recalls a particular Spring Break that was especially gratifying. Mullen has José's blessing.

Will Muschamp- José is conflicted by this Muschamp. He has coached under two people that José finds distasteful, Nick Saban and the coach whose name shall not be spoken. But José also recognizes that people sometimes make mistakes in judgment (see José's wives 1, 2, and 3) and that given the right circumstances, can change. For example, José feels that should wife #4 turn out to be Jessica Alba, then he will be a loving and devoted husband.

Mike McIntyre- McIntyre graduated from the Georgia Institute of Technology which has a silly bumblebee mascot. Also, José once received a speeding ticket in Georgia where he was racially profiled and therefore cannot support the candidacy of this McIntyre character.

Houston Nutt- The coach from Arkansas is an emotional rollercoaster. José likes rollercoasters. His favorite is the Sheikra at Busch Gardens which involves a 90 degree drop and some wild loops, twists and turns. Following José's favorite team has seemed more like the Freefall ride than the Sheikra lately.

My name is José Valdez IV and these are my thoughts.

Notes:
- After getting a few encouraging responses to my initial thoughts, this one seemed to be very well received. At this point I figured I might have something that a few people would be interested in.
- I did like the idea of Rick Neuheisel as head coach, but was concerned that he would go back to the West Coast the first opportunity he had. He ended up getting the UCLA job a short time later.
- Newcastle is a great beer.

- Muschamp was later named "Head Coach in Waiting" or some such thing that means he'll be the coach at Texas when Mack Brown leaves.

- It is amazing that Mullen was even in the conversation as a potential candidate. I doubt he was even contacted about the possibility of getting the Ole Miss job. I can't believe that I wrote that he had my blessing. I obviously didn't do enough research.

- Despite my negative comment concerning McIntyre, I like him and actually played a year of Junior High football with him in Oxford when his father was on Steve Sloan's staff.

- The reference to the bumblebee mascot comes from a time my mom happened to walk in the room while a Georgia Tech game was on television. She exclaimed, "What are they? The bumblebees?"

José's Thoughts on Coach Nutt

The lyrics of a certain British band summarize José's feelings about the hiring of Coach Houston Nutt:

It's the Honky Tonk Women (yeah)
Give me, give me, give me, the honky tonk blues

Wait a second. That is not the correct song. José profusely apologizes for this lapse. Most of his time is spent alternately thinking about Ole Miss sports and honky tonk women. The lyrics José intended to quote were:

You can't always get what you want
But if you try sometimes, well you might find
You get what you need

José admits that Coach Nutt was not his first choice. Johnny Vaught rising like a Tucson from the ashes was his first choice. So José did not get what he wanted. José did get what he needed though, a coach who is alive (this should always be the first requirement, as the schools that have attempted to bypass this step have failed miserably), who has experience leading a team in a major conference (and José considers the SEC the only major conference), and who will bring excitement and enthusiasm to the program. As José stated in his thoughts on the candidates, Coach Nutt is an emotional rollercoaster, and José likes rollercoasters.

What José feels is missing is a good nickname for Coach Nutt. There are too many obvious references to his last name, all of which José finds distasteful. Much like José found the Miller Lite advertisement with the two buxom women wrestling in the water fountain distasteful all 347 times he watched it (José has Tivo). But José recognizes that perhaps the administration of our school had a master plan in hiring Coach Nutt, one that would save its fans a lot of money. A lot of people are driving around with "O" The Coach stickers on their vehicles. Well, Coach Nutt's first name begins with "H" "O", so rather than having to print entirely new stickers, all that needs to be done is to add an "H" to the front of the current ones. "Coach HO".

After saying that out loud a couple of times José thinks that that is perhaps not the best idea. José freely admits that not all of his ideas are great ones. He recalls one instance where he had the idea to make out with his best friend's girlfriend. That was a particularly bad idea, one which José definitely regrets, but if you had seen her…

My name is José Valdez IV and these are my thoughts.

Notes:

- I was very excited about the hiring of Houston Nutt and actually could not believe how things fell into place for Ole Miss. Just a few days prior, we were as miserable a fan base as could be. Then all of a sudden a proven SEC head coach fell into our laps. Things were looking up.

- Ironically, I had written a post comparing Nutt to Cutcliffe a few years earlier (pre- José) where I stated that I preferred the even-keel approach of Cutcliffe to that of the emotional Nutt. I felt Nutt would not be able to sustain that style over a long period of time. It was not the first time I was mistaken.

- I am aware that it is actually a Phoenix that rises from the ashes.

José's Thoughts on Troy

Let José be the first to admit that he is not as well-versed in the history of Troy and the intricacies of their battle with the ancient Sigma Chi's (or was it Phi Delts?, José is not certain). What he does know is that the Trojans could not have been particularly smart to accept the gift of a giant horse from the Sigma Chi's (led by Brad Pitt), who had been laying siege to the city for ten years. By the way, this is where we get the saying "Beware of Sigma Chi's bearing gifts." (Again, if it was actually Phi Delts José offers his sincere apology). It is hard for José to fear a team that once fell for such a ruse. But in case you were not aware the whole story of the Battle of Troy is the work of Homer and purported to be legend. José does not believe in legends… unless you consider Bigfoot a legend. José most certainly believes in Bigfoot.

Anyway, José thought it would be a great idea to wheel a giant horse onto the floor tonight before tipoff as an offering to our visitors from Alabama. When the starting lineups were introduced out could come the Rebel starting five, led by Kenny Williams of course. José suggested this very idea to Coach Kennedy. Coach Kennedy called José a &*#@ and told him to get lost. José loves Coach Kennedy.

José digresses for a moment to address the question on everyone's mind. Regarding Mr. Brad Pitt, where exactly does José stand on the Jennifer Anniston/Angelina Jolie debate? Let José clearly state that he falls on the Anniston side, but can sympathize with Mr. Pitt. José found himself in a similar situation in his younger days. When it came time to choose between the classically beautiful Camila (Anniston) and the sexy but frightening Isabel (Jolie) for his first wife, José did not choose wisely. Alas, Isabel left José after a few shorts months, taking their three adopted Myanmar children with her and Camila still does not return José's calls.

Regarding the Rebel opponents, Troy basketball is perhaps best known for a game in 1992 against DeVry in which it scored 258 points, including 51 three-pointers. One ordinarily might be impressed by such a feat, but if José also told you that he and four of his amigos played the Fighting Computer Technicians of DeVry that same year, after drinking tequila all night, and lost by one point (when José missed the front end of a one and one with two seconds left), then perhaps you would not be so impressed. José believes the Rebels will fare much better against Troy than he and his amigos did so many years before, assuming there is no tequila involved.

My name is José Valdez IV and these are my thoughts.

Notes:

- **This was the fifth game of the basketball season, but since I had written a few thoughts, I thought I would at least attempt to write something for each of the remaining games during the season.**

- **Brad Pitt starred in the movie *Troy*.**

- **I get a little more into the personal history of José in this one, revealing his belief in Bigfoot, propensity for tequila consumption and his great affection for Coach Kennedy. Those would prove to be recurring themes.**

Jose's Random Thoughts

José has many thoughts on things other than honky tonk women and his "counselor" tells him that it is sometimes good to share them.

Regarding Coach Nutt's plans to put names back on the jerseys: José agrees 100% with this decision. In fact, José wishes everyone had their names on their shirts. José does. This would eliminate those awkward moments when someone who José cannot remember their name greets him and José invariably responds, "Hey … Amigo … How's it going?" José freely admits that his memory is not very good. For example, he cannot recall anything that transpired between September 2 and 5, while he was in Las Vegas.

On Global Warming: Let's see, the hotter it is, the skimpier the outfits are on Ole Miss coeds. This is a bad thing? José is currently letting his car idle in the driveway with the hope of raising the temperature of the earth at least one degree.

Concerning the accusations that José has a man-crush on Andy Kennedy: José categorically denies these scurrilous accusations. Just because José obsesses night and day about what Coach Kennedy has in store for the next opponent, how many minutes he's getting the newcomers, what he's doing on the recruiting trail, how many championships he's going to win, and how Ole Miss can hold on to him, does not mean he has a man-crush on him. José does admit that he has had a recurring dream about Coach Kennedy lately. In the dream José is a guard on the basketball team and misses a wide open lay-up in the waning seconds against the team whose name shall not be spoken. José leaves town in the dark of the night to escape the wrath of Coach Kennedy, but just like Javier Bardem in *No Country for Old Men*, Kennedy tracks José down. The dream ends the same way every time. Coach Kennedy flips a coin and says "Call it … friendo." And José wakes up in a pool of sweat.

On Doyle Jackson: José hopes that Javier Bardem (or Coach Kennedy) catches up with him eventually.

My name is José Valdez IV and these are my thoughts.

Notes:

- **In retrospect, I shouldn't have written this one. It was early on in the José process and I probably should have paced myself a little more. This one wasn't necessary.**

José's Thoughts on New Mexico

José knows what you are thinking. Who will José root for when the Rebels play against New Mexico? You should be ashamed for even thinking such a thing. Of course José will be for Ole Miss. He much preferred the old Mexico to this newer version. The whole "New" Mexico seems contrived by some advertising agency to drum up new business. "Come visit the "New" Mexico and see what changes we have made!" Or "Mexico! Now under new management!" No, José will not be duped by such as this.

There are some interesting things about this New Mexico that José must acknowledge. John Madden is from there. José likes his video games. José particularly enjoys beating his friends at Madden and then rubbing it in their faces. (24-20 Jorge. Take that you filthy swine. You son of a motherless goat!) José's first wife did not like Mr. Madden's video games. In addition to John Madden, former Indy car racer Al Unser is from New Mexico. Ironically, former Indy car racer Bobby Unser is also from New Mexico. What are the odds? People apparently like to drive fast in New Mexico.

One thing José must admit is that this New Mexico basketball team plays in an arena with a much better nickname than the Ole Miss one does. The Lobos' arena is called "The Pit" because it was dug down into the ground. It has gained the reputation as one of the most difficult places for opponents to play and also hosted the memorable 1983 national championship game between the N.C. State Wolfpack and the Houston Cougars. This game is well-known for the scene after the upset when the N.C. State coach, Jim Valvano ran around the court, supposedly looking for someone to hug. José has long felt that Valvano was actually running around looking for a particular brunette cheerleader to tongue-kiss. Alas, he was unable to locate the cheerleader among the throng and had to settle for an awkward man-hug with Thurl Bailey. You may say, "But José, Valvano would have never done such a thing. The television cameras would have caught it all and he would have been in serious trouble with the wife." This could have easily been explained away as an incident that occurred in the excitement of the moment. *Note: That is exactly the explanation that José used to wife #1 for his tongue-kiss with the women sitting next to him at the 1983 Egg Bowl. She did not buy it so perhaps it is best that Valvano could not locate said cheerleader.*

Regarding the nickname of Ole Miss's basketball arena, José does not like "The Tad Pad" and never refers to it as such. Tad Smith suffices. Who is responsible for this deplorable nick-name? After all, has anyone since the 1970's referred to a home or building as a "pad"? José thinks not. In fact, José's advice to you is that if anyone you know invites you to go to a game with them at "The Tad Pad" you should immediately run away, because chances are they also want to swap wives with you. Now if your wife favors Rosie O'Donnell and your friend's wife most closely resembles Salma Hayek, well then perhaps…

For those who were not aware, the coach of New Mexico is Steve Alford, former Indiana great and until recently the head coach at Iowa. José used to be a big fan of Alford. That is because they were both members of an exclusive club, the club for men who are 35 years-old or older and continue to part their hair in the middle. Two or three years ago Alford discontinued this practice and began slicking his hair back. *Note: This was around the same time he sold his Trans Am.* José lost all respect for Alford and hopes the Rebels destroy his Lobos. José plans to be there to witness the thrashing. If you see a fan taunting the New Mexico coach while holding a comb, that could be José. Or it could just be another disgruntled member of the club.

My name is José Valdez IV and these are my thoughts.

Notes:

- **I believe this is the first one that got a response from a fan of the other team. A New Mexico fan apparently saw it on the Spirit Board and enjoyed it, vowing to root for Ole Miss against all their future opponents.**

- **John Madden is actually from Minnesota, not New Mexico. A fact my research staff should have caught.**

- This is Jorge's first appearance in any of the thoughts. The derogatory comments José directs at him come from the movie *Three Amigos*, one of my favorites.

- I really do hate it when people call Tad Smith Coliseum "The Tad Pad".

- Yes, I parted my hair in the middle, but only in the early 1980's. I'm fully prepared to return to that look though if it comes back in style.

José's Thoughts on Central Florida

Saturday the Rebels face the Central Florida Knights of Columbus. UCF is in Orlando, Florida which is better known as the home of theme parks such as Disney World, Universal Studios, and Sea World. As José has stated previously, he is a rollercoaster guy, so he prefers Universal's Islands of Adventure. Also, José is still fuming over Disney World's removal of his favorite attraction, Mr. Toad's Wild Ride. A shot of tequila was the perfect setup for that ride. That was one crazy toad as José recalls.

There is a bitter debate among many Central Florida alums as to who their most distinguished graduate is: Mark Miller, the lead singer for the country music band Sawyer Brown, or Angelo Garcia, singer/songwriter for the 1980's pop band Menudo. José thinks you know which direction he would lean toward if he had a Chihuahua in that fight. Menudo was the Beatles of Mexico. José offers you a sample of their lyrics:

> *If you're not here, by my side*
> *Can't hold back the tears*
> *I try to hide*
> *Don't think I can take it*
> *I know I won't make it*
> *Make it without you*

How does one top such as that?

One of the leading players for the Knights of Columbus is Kenrick Zondervan, who is from Hoofddorp, Holland. You can certainly understand José's animosity towards a team which includes a player from The Netherlands. Yes, it is indeed because of the Dutch Rebellion against the Habsburgs. As far as José is concerned, Zondervan is a modern day

15

William of Orange and although he does not wish for young Kenrick to meet the same fate that William did, it would not bother José if he twisted an ankle.

José knows what you are thinking. You are thinking that perhaps José has been smoking something that is legal in Dutch cities but not here in America. That is not the case. If you think José has strange thoughts now, imagine what they might be like if he partook of illegal substances. No, José sticks with the tequila. In fact, he lives his life according to three basic tenets (two of which he obtained from the philosopher Navin R. Johnson):

> Say no to drugs
> Lord loves a workin' man
> Don't trust whitey

The world would be a better place if everyone joined José in practicing these basic concepts.

Regarding the actual game, José is anxious to see how the Rebels respond in their first road game of the year. With so many freshman logging significant minutes the game should serve as a barometer of what we can expect early in SEC play. *Note: Jose is not sure that last sentence makes sense but has been determined to work "barometer" into his posts for some time and it seemed like a good opportunity.*

José thinks the kids respond. Also, José hears Coach Kennedy doesn't like Florida (have you ever seen him with a tan?), thinks Menudo were sissies, and is chagrined by the Treaty of Münster. Rebels 84 Knights of Columbus 77.

My name is José Valdez IV and these are my thoughts.

Notes:
- **I took the family to Disney World numerous times while we lived in Tampa and am still bitter that they removed Mr. Toad's Wild Ride.**
- **Of course the Navin R. Johnson quote is from the movie *The Jerk*. The principles are sound.**

José's Thoughts on His Best Ole Miss Experience

José has seen the banter on the message board where people have shared their favorite Ole Miss sports experiences so he thought he would weigh in on his favorite.

This was not an easy decision for José because he was at Auburn in 1999 when the Rebels defeated The Coach Whose Name Shall Not Be Spoken. That was particularly enjoyable and much tequila was consumed afterwards. José recorded the game and must have watched the final play twenty times that night on his VCR. *Note: This was before Tivo: the greatest advancement in civilization in the past 100 years.*

For José's favorite Ole Miss sports experience he must take you back to the year 1986. José was a much younger man and he had recently purchased a white cotton jacket which he wore on a daily basis over various colored t-shirts. José thought he would have babes for days. Seven years later he finally threw in the towel when he realized that Ole Miss girls just weren't that into Miami Vice. *Note: Miami Vice was cancelled in early 1990.* Even though he gave up on the Miami Vice look, José has not forsaken the hair-parted-in the-middle look to this day. Steve Alford may have succumbed to peer pressure, but as long as Mark Richt continues to stand with José, he will continue to rock that hair.

Please pardon José for his digression. Anyway, it was 1986 and José and his best amigos, Jorge and Paco, decided to take a road trip to Baton Rouge, Louisiana to see the underdog Rebels take on the top ten LSU Tigers. José was the designated driver while Jorge and Paco sat in the back drinking the cheapest beer that could be found in the store. What sticks in José's mind about the drive was how many times "Word Up" played on the radio. Up until that time José liked the song (although he preferred "Alligator Woman"), but listening to Jorge and Paco sing it ruined it for him. Don't ask about Jorge and Paco's version of "True Colors".

It was José's first time in Tiger Stadium and let him say that it was not a friendly place, especially if you are wearing a white cotton jacket over a fuchsia t-shirt. The people said many uncomplimentary things about José's team, clothing, hair and ancestry. But all of that is forgotten if your team wins the game and that is what José's Rebels did that day. He cannot recall all of the events, but remembers J.R. Ambrose having a great game, a key goal-line stand, and the potential game winning field goal being pushed wide to the left. José has not felt such euphoria since. Just as at the 1983 Egg Bowl, José kissed the closest female he could find. This is a safe thing to do if you are sitting among Ole Miss fans. José does not recommend trying this if you are among LSU fans. Anyway, she was apparently happy about the game as well. Her boyfriend, not so much.

It was a good day and a good year. The Rebels went to a bowl game. Willie Morris was alive and well and writer-in-residence at Ole Miss. *Note: Jose regrets to this day never approaching him at the Gin and sharing a drink with him. Perhaps Willie would have advised José that the Miami Vice look was never going to catch on in Mississippi.*

My name is José Valdez IV and these are my thoughts.

Notes:

- Perhaps I used a little hyperbole when I made the comment about Tivo being the greatest advancement in civilization of the last 100 years. But it's at least top five.

- The "rock that hair" comment was in reference to a certain TSWNSNBS signee stating that part of the reason he chose them was that they promised him the number he wanted and he could "rock that two".

- The 1986 trip to Tiger Stadium was my first trip there. I've been to five games now and the Rebels have won three of them. It will be difficult to ever top that first one.

- It really is one of my life's biggest regrets that I didn't spend some time with Willie Morris while I was in school.

José's Thoughts on His Worst Ole Miss Sports Experience

Unfortunately if you have been a fan of Ole Miss sports for the past thirty years or so and have been to many athletic contests, there are quite a few to choose from when it comes to worst experience. Various Alabama football games (Thanks Doyle!) and Super Regionals would have to rank high on any list. For José it basically came down to two choices. Coming in 2nd was the 1999 Egg Bowl. *Note: José did not attend this year's contest which is probably a good thing.* José became physically ill after that football game. The walk down from the upper deck was unbelievably miserable and if José had been carrying a weapon he would have left a swath of destruction that Javier Bardem could have only dreamed about. *Note: José is only speaking in hyperbole. He is really not a violent man and has never hurt anyone (except a dog once, and that was by accident...oh and Aunt Edna).*

But the choice for José's worst Ole Miss sports experience is really an easy one and can be summarized in two words: Val Po. Yes, José was there to experience the tragedy that was the Valparaiso game. Only those who ventured to Oklahoma City for that game can fully understand the depth of despondency that filled the Ole Miss section. José knows that those watching or listening felt bad also, but at least you did not have to immediately drive 500 friggin miles back home with Jorge and Paco afterwards. *Note: Jorge cried the entire way, Paco hurled various profanities at no one in particular, and José sat mumbling incoherently in the back seat.*

José came to realize that there are different levels of misery and he would like to share them with you. They start at the easiest to overcome and proceed to the most difficult.

- Losing one's job at the 7-Eleven
- Losing one's girlfriend to the guy at Subway
- Losing a contest to have lunch with Salma Hayek
- Losing the last bottle of tequila
- Losing one's life in a tragic gardening accident
- Losing to Valpo on a shot by Bryce *#$&% Drew

After that José felt that life as an Ole Miss fan was too difficult to continue. He cursed the day that José III took him to his first Rebel game and vowed never to subject himself to such misery in the future. Eventually José came to realize that hey, was it over when the Germans bombed Pearl Harbor? *Note: Jose congratulates himself for being the first person to consider using the ancient Animal House reference on the Ole Miss Spirit Message Board.* No, it was not over. There would be good times ahead, times of joy when many beautiful senoritas would want to celebrate championships with José in the hot tub. José hopes that Coach Nutt, Coach Kennedy or Coach Bianco will bring him a championship soon and is heating up the hot tub now.

My name is José Valdez IV and these are my thoughts.

Notes:

- **The references to hurting the dog and Aunt Edna of course come from the movie *Vacation*.**
- **I did attend the Valpo game with two good friends. The drive home was not that dissimilar from how I describe it in the thoughts.**
- **The tragic gardening accident reference comes from the classic movie *This is Spinal Tap*.**
- **The "Germans bomb Pearl Harbor" line from *Animal House* has become the standard reply on the Ole Miss Spirit Message Board whenever someone posts something purported to be news, but that everyone else already knows about. Invariably, someone who has never seen the movie responds with "It was the Japanese that bombed Pearl Harbor!" It never gets old though and always cracks me up.**

José's Thoughts on Ole Miss Basketball

José has previously stated that he has been having a recurring dream that Andy Kennedy was hunting him down like a dog after José missed a layup and cost the Rebels a game against The Team Whose Name Shall Not Be Spoken. Well, it appears that José is having more dreams about Coach Kennedy and the Ole Miss basketball program. *Note: You may add these dreams to the list of José's other recurring dreams: the one where he goes to school naked, and the one where he is in an underground parking garage being chased by the bad gorillas from Planet of the Apes.* In José's most recent dream he is as light as the ether, and is floating over a basketball arena watching the Rebel basketball team celebrate some kind of championship. What year is it? Is it an SEC Tournament Championship? A trip to the Final Four? Possibly even a National Championship? José is not sure because he cannot get close enough to tell, or is perhaps afraid that Coach Kennedy will jab him with the scissors he was using to cut down the nets.

José is giving fair warning now, if you are not already on the bandwagon, get on soon because there won't be much room before long. Just as you would be frowned upon by Boston fans if you bought you first Red Sox cap within the last month, you will be by Rebel basketball fans if you wait to start coming to games after the team is a recognized power. *Note: In addition to the timing, it is also important to be selective as to which bandwagons you jump on. For example, you would not have wanted to jump on the Wham! bandwagon in the mid 1980's. Trust José on this one.*

Many good Ole Miss basketball moments have been experienced by José over the years. He began his Rebel fandom watching John Stroud play. José was there for the greatest game ever played at Tad Smith (not The Tad

Pad), the overtime victory over LSU when Chris Jackson scored 55 points and Gerald Glass added 53 of his own. That was also the night Jorge and Paco got into a fight over who was the greater Russian Novelist: Tolstoy or Dostoevsky. Jorge was adamant that it was Tolstoy while Paco insisted it was Dostoevsky. *Note: José understands Jorge's argument. After all, War and Peace is epic, but José sides with Paco on this one, believing the combined weight of Crime and Punishment along with The Brothers Karamazov is greater than War and Peace and Anna Karenina. Still, José kept his mouth shut. Jorge is a biter.* After many punches, kicks, bites, and some bloodshed, Jorge and Paco agreed to disagree.

Once again, José apologizes for the digression. The point he was trying to make is that he has witnessed many good Ole Miss basketball moments, the earlier mentioned ones, along with various SEC Western Division Championships. He was even there for the Sweet Sixteen appearance in San Antonio. *Note: They have very good tequila in San Antonio, and José partook of his share.* Those were all good moments. José believes there are great moments ahead in the very near future. Ole Miss has had some very good basketball players in its history. It has also had a few great athletes. It has never had as many good basketball players who are also great athletes as it has right now. This is going to continue to improve in the future. This team will go through some growing pains, as any team that relies on so much youth would be expected to, but José expects them to be playing games in February that will determine whether they are an NCAA team or not. In another year or two, José expects them to be playing for much more than that.

People of Jackson and the surrounding countryside, make plans to go see the Rebels play Thursday night against Winthrop. You won't regret it (as José regrets his wasted Miami Vice years, the cancellation of "What's Happening?", wife #3, and the two hours of his life he lost at the movie theater watching *Hudson Hawk*).

My name is José Valdez IV and these are my thoughts.

Notes:

- **I think just about everyone has the dream about going to school (or some public place) naked. I'm not so sure that anyone else has the *Planet of the Apes* dream that I have. This one usually occurs every five years or so now.**

- **The "light as the ether" comment comes from *Raising Arizona*.**

- This thought included the first hint that I'm a Red Sox fan.
- This is also the first mention of a fight between Jorge and Paco.
- There will never be a more exciting game played at Tad Smith Coliseum than the Ole Miss-LSU game of 1989. The Rebels won 113-112. I carried the ticket stub in my wallet for a few years and while at The Gin one night, got it signed by Gerald Glass and Tim Jumper.

José's Thoughts on Winthrop

Winthrop University is in Rock Hill, South Carolina and was founded in 1886. It was named for Robert C. Winthrop.

"José , Why was it named for Mr. Winthrop?" you ask.

Because Mr. Winthrop was the first person to donate money for the building of the college.

"Wow José. This Winthrop sounds like he was a very generous man. I know it was 1886, but he still must have given a lot of money. How much did he give? $100,000? $200,000?"

What is this? Twenty Questions? Anyway, José was about to tell you that Mr. Winthrop gave the exorbitant sum of $1,500.

Now José admits that any gift to a college is a generous one, but does that mean you get the college named after you just by being the first to make a donation? If so, where does José sign up?

Based on that information José intends to start a college. Money is tight for José now after the "incident" with the receptionist at his former place of employment, but he feels he can pony up $200 to start the José Valdez IV Institute of Technology (José Tech). Those of you willing to join José can have buildings and streets named after you (first come first served). José has not settled on a nickname yet for José Tech, but has narrowed the possibilities to:

- Cuervos (José feels that needs no explanation)

- Fighting Chimichangas (Celebrates the heritage of José's people while still inspiring fear)

- Flood (Hopefully not as offensive as some other name José could have chosen)

- Hickory Huskers (José loves "Hoosiers")
- Salma Hayeks (If she agrees to a few personal appearances this is the clear-cut favorite)
- Angels of Anaheim

Concerning the Winthrop basketball program, it is a good one. The Iron Eagles 2 have been to six of the last eight NCAA tournaments and the team was ranked in the top twenty-five in the country for the first time in its history this past season. Although the current team is only 5-3, they frighten José. Not as much as the Kappa he took to a football game his sophomore year, but they do frighten him. *Note: José does not hold this one "weekend from hell" against the entire Kappa Kappa Gamma organization. He recognizes that the vast majority of them are not raving lunatics and that perhaps "Carmen" had just had a bad week. Of course José understands that it is entirely possible that she was perfectly normal and that José may have been the crazy one. In his experience, José has found that tequila sometimes has an impact on José's behavior... and memory.*

José is excited about the game being played in Jackson, although he was there the last time the Rebels played a game in Jackson, and that was not so good. As José recalls, Southwestern Louisiana (now The University of Louisiana- Marquis de Lafayette) had a player who shot about 117% from the floor and even Gerald Glass could not prevent the Rebels from losing. The only good news of the evening was that José went to The Dock afterwards. José also believes that was the night he was introduced to Jello shots. José likes Jello and José also likes shots. It seemed like the best combination since chocolate and peanut better so why not give it a try? He must admit that they were quite delicious. José can offer his endorsement, if you partake of them in moderation. *Note: Jose did not.* If someone offers you a Jello pudding shot though, José recommends you decline.

The other thing José recalls about the evening is that Jorge and Paco got into a fight over who was hotter, Belinda Carlisle of the Go Go's or Susanna Hoffs of The Bangles. Paco was adamant that it was Belinda while Jorge insisted it was Susanna. *Note: José sided with Jorge, but kept his mouth shut. Paco is an eye-gouger. If you ever saw the "Walk Like an Egyptian" video, the way Susanna cut her eyes (she looked right at José) and bit her lip, then you would understand why José agreed with Jorge .* After many punches, kicks, bites, and some bloodshed, Jorge and Paco agreed to disagree.

José believes Coach Kennedy will have the Rebels ready to take on Robert C. Winthrop University. Rebels-81 Iron Eagles 2-67.

My name is José Valdez IV and these are my thoughts.

Notes:

- **This is the second mention of Salma Hayek in one of my thoughts. She would prove to be a recurring theme as well.**
- **I did take a crazy person to a football game, but it was not my sophomore year and she was not a Kappa.**
- **Yes, I am partial towards the lead singer of the Bangles. My college roommate and I would often yell "Bangles check!" which required that you turn the television to MTV to see if the "Walk Like an Egyptian" video happened to be playing. I've matured since then.**

José's Thoughts on DePaul

José does not understand the necessity of placing "De" in front of "Paul" in the Chicago University's name. He feels it is pretentious and was tempted to refer to himself as "DeJosé" throughout the remainder of his thoughts as a form of protest, but will choose to refrain from doing so. José is well known for his ability to refrain from almost anything...except temptation.

DePaul is perhaps best-known as Gillian Anderson's alma mater. Miss Anderson was "Scully" on the X-Files. José loved the X-Files. That is he loved the show until the episode about El Chupacabra. This is the legendary creature, which mostly preys on goats. It drains all of the blood from its victims and all of José's people know the creature to be real. José's older sister, Carmelita, and her boyfriend disappeared from the Valdez village when José was a young boy. José III informed all that they were taken by El Chupacabra. José does not believe the rumors that they were seen in El Paso on many occasions after their disappearance. Anyway, that episode hit too close to home and caused José to have many nightmares. *Note: They were not as frequent as the going to school naked, being chased by gorillas from the Planet of the Apes, and Coach Kennedy trying to kill José, but occurred often enough to upset him.*

What José did not know going into this game was who DePaul University was named for? There were certainly some likely candidates named Paul who it would be no surprise to anyone were they to have a college named for them as a tribute to their greatness. José offers you a few possibilities and his thoughts on whether they could be the Paul who the school was named for:

- Paul Revere- The great patriot who rode through the Massachusetts countryside proclaiming "the British are coming" would appear to be a likely candidate. When you also consider that he later started a band, Paul Revere and the Raiders, who recorded such hits as "Indian Reservation" and "Kicks" then you would think he would be the front-runner for having a college named for him.

- Paul Orndorff- José was a fan of the great wrestler Orndorff. He still recalls the anger he felt when Jerry Lawler threw a powdery substance into Orndorff's face, blinding him for a few weeks. It is amazing that Orndorff was able to recover and eventually continue his wrestling career. Someone like that should be celebrated by having a college named for him. Orndorff is a very likely candidate.

- Paul McCartney- Entirely possible, but José thinks if the school were named after a Beatle it would be DeRingo.

- Paul Bunyan- The legendary lumberjack, who along with his blue ox, Babe, wandered the state of Minnesota felling trees and such. José does not think it likely that DePaul was named after Paul Bunyan because they would be the Blue Oxen rather than Blue Demons. Also, José doubts the school would be named for a legendary character. José reminds you that legends are not real, except for Bigfoot … and El Chupacabra.

- The Apostle Paul- If DePaul had originally been named DeSaul it would be clear that this was who the school was named for. Since that is not the case, José must look elsewhere for the answer.

What is that you say? The school is named for the 17th century French priest Saint Vincent de Paul? That is very bad news for José. He can think of nothing remotely interesting to say about this man. But José does respect the Catholic priest, even though José is not himself a practitioner of the Catholic faith. The Catholics do not judge José for his consumption of tequila, which he appreciates.

One thing José must admit has bothered him over the years is the proclivity for schools that were originally founded as "Christian" colleges to name their mascots after members of the nether region. Wake Forest (Baptist) is the Demon Deacons; Duke (founded by Methodists and Quakers) is the Blue Devils. DePaul's nickname is of course, the Blue Demons. José wonders what their second choice was? Disciples of Beelzebub?

José has bad memories of this DePaul. He recalls an NIT game from the 1983 that had the Rebels won, would have sent them to Madison Square Garden for the Final Four. That night is also memorable because it was the night Jorge and Paco got into a fight over who was the greater country singer, George Jones or Johnny Cash. Jorge insisted it was Jones while Paco was adamant that Cash was greater. *Note: José sided with Paco on this one. While he believes "He Stopped Loving Her Today" is the greatest country song ever, Cash's body of work ("Boy Named Sue", "Ring of Fire", "Folsom Prison Blues", etc.) tips the scales in his favor. But José kept his mouth shut. Jorge is a biter.* After many punches, kicks, bites, and some bloodshed, Jorge and Paco agreed to disagree.

José believes that Coach Kennedy will have the Rebels ready to exact revenge for that game twenty-four years ago. Rebels 82 Disciples of Beelzebub 77.

My name is José Valdez IV and these are my thoughts.

Notes:

- I was excited about the Rebels playing DePaul as I really liked the Blue Demon teams when I was young. Mark Aguirre, Terry Cummings, Teddy Grubbs and others were great basketball players and fun to watch. I also recall them suffering a Valpo-esque loss in the NCAA Tourney one year to St. Joseph's when they were ranked #1 in the country.

- Yes, I was a big *X-Files* fan and this is my first mention of El Chupacabra. He would show up every so often in later thoughts.

- This was also the first mention of Jerry Lawler. I watched the wrestling out of Memphis as a kid, so was a big fan (when he was the good guy. I hated him when he was the bad guy).

José's Thoughts on La Salle

José has difficulty suppressing his feelings about the fraud that is La Salle athletics. There have been many frauds perpetrated on the American public over the years which include:

- The staged landing of a man on the moon. José thinks everyone is well aware that Van Allen radiation belts, solar rays, and Coronal Mass Ejections make such a thing impossible.

- The famous picture of "Bigfoot" taken while he was walking across a clearing in the forest. That wasn't the real Bigfoot. The real Bigfoot is much hairier and wears a cape.

- The crop circles in England that were supposedly created by aliens were later discovered to have been cut by Sigma Nu's on a pledge trip.

- On a more personal note, José's online girlfriend of the last six months, "Consuela", who turned out to be a dude. *Note: José should not be faulted for this as the pictures that were sent to him were gorgeous. After the fact Jorge pointed out to José that these were actually pictures of Kathleen Turner in "Body Heat". Unfortunately José's village did not have HBO in the 1980's and he did not see this masterpiece of the cinema until it was far too late. (It now has "Save Until I Delete" status on his Tivo.)*

None of these compare to the fraudulency that is La Salle athletics though.

"Why is this so José?" you ask. José will tell you.

René Robert Cavelier, Sieur de La Salle, was born in Rouen, Normandy in 1643. As a young man he was briefly a member of the Jesuit order, that is until he was released after citing "moral weaknesses" (José is right there with you René Robert). To La Salle's credit he did not let this get him down. After relocating to what is now Canada, he became interested in finding a water passage west to China. Although he obviously never found this passage, he did lead many expeditions in the Great Lakes region and down the Mississippi (where he supposedly dined at Cock of the Walk in Natchez). Eventually La Salle was killed by mutineers on one of his expeditions when it was discovered that he had been hording strombolis in his tent.

"That is interesting José," you say. "So that is where they get the nickname Explorers?"

This is where the fraud comes in. THE SCHOOL WAS NOT NAMED FOR RENE ROBERT CAVALIER, SIEUR DE LA SALLE, IT WAS NAMED FOR ST. JEAN-BAPTISTE DE LA SALLE!!!!!!

Jean-Baptiste de la Salle was a French priest who was known for his educating of the poor. When it came time to name their athletic teams, apparently this wasn't good enough for the people of La Salle University and they decided to go with the exciting explorer guy.

Don't get him wrong, José is all about lying when necessary. For example when wife #1 asked him whether a certain dress made her look fat, it might have been prudent for José to lie, but alas he did not (hence the necessity for wife #2). José also chose to lie about his age in order to get a fake id when he was younger (but that was just so he could vote). José cannot condone what the teams of La Salle University have been doing for their entire history though. A line must be drawn somewhere.

The only thing José can say he likes about La Salle is that Peter Boyle went to school there. Most will remember him as Frank on *Everybody Loves Raymond*, but José remembers him most fondly as the monster in *Young Frankenstein*. He still recalls the evening he went to see the movie. That was the night Jorge and Paco got into a fight over who should have won the 1941 American League MVP Award. Jorge insisted it should have been Ted Williams, while Paco was adamant the selection of Joe DiMaggio was the correct one. *Note: José sided with Jorge on this one. While DiMaggio's 56-game hitting streak was impressive, he had nowhere near the stats of Williams that year (.406 BA, 37 HR, 120 RBI). Still José kept quiet. Paco is an eye-gouger.* After many punches, kicks, and some bloodshed, Jorge and Paco agreed to disagree.

José thinks Coach Kennedy will have the boys ready to play. Rebels-89 Lying Liars of La Salle-80.

My name is José Valdez IV and these are my thoughts.

Notes:

- The staged landing of a man on the moon reference is in honor of my wife's grandfather, who didn't buy into the government propaganda.

- The information I discovered about the Explorer nickname being given after the wrong La Salle was just too good to pass up. You couldn't make up something like that.

- Getting a fake ID in order to vote is straight from *The Breakfast Club*.

- I really do think Ted Williams was robbed in the 1941 American League MVP voting.

José's Thoughts on Clemson

It makes things difficult for José when the Rebels play games three days in a row. While he enjoys thinking about DePaul, LaSalle, and Clemson, José is accustomed to having somewhat of a break to think about normal everyday things including, but not limited to:

- How can the Rebels manage to hold on to Coach Kennedy for the next twenty-five years?
- Should one drink tequila before beer or visa versa?
- What color sweater would Coach Kennedy like for Christmas?
- Does Salma Hayek like men who part their hair in the middle?
- What is Coach Kennedy's favorite vacation spot?
- What sort of predicament will Jack Bauer find himself in on next season's *24*?
- Does Coach Kennedy like tequila as much as José?
- Why is Pluto no longer classified as a planet?
- What is Coach Kennedy's favorite vegetable?
- Who made the decision to cancel *Mama's Family*?
- Why doesn't Coach Kennedy return José's calls?

These are the kinds of things that roll through José's head on a daily basis, but he must turn his thoughts to Clemson.

For many years José has felt favorably towards Clemson University. There was nothing to particularly dislike about the school or program.

That is until José discovered how the school originated. Apparently the founder of the school, Thomas Green Clemson, left most of his estate to establish a college. This is admirable in José's opinion. But then it goes bad. Mr. Clemson left specific instructions in his will that the school be modeled after a certain school in Mississippi whose name shall not be spoken. Yes, you heard José correctly. José has racked his brain trying to understand the thought process that went into this. He thinks it must have gone something like this.

> Wow. That Starkville Sure is a lovely place.
> They sure do have great cheese there.
> I want my school to be just like the one located there.

This is strikingly similar to the thought process José had one night at the Warehouse.

> I really haven't had that much tequila.
> I'm going to hit on the next good-looking girl I see.
> Boy, that Rebel defensive lineman Mike Fitzsimmons' girlfriend sure is hot.

This Clemson team will be the toughest test the Rebels have faced to date. They are also unbeaten and ranked 15ᵗʰ in the country. José has very bad memories of the night the Tigers knocked the Rebels out of the NIT last year. That night was also memorable because Jorge and Paco got into a fight over who the better TV detective was, Kojak or Columbo? Jorge insisted it was Kojak while Paco was adamant that Columbo was the better of the two. *Note: José sided with Paco on this one. He loved the cat and mouse game Columbo always played with the suspect. But José kept his mouth shut. Jorge is a biter.*

José believes that Coach Kennedy will have the boys ready for Clemson. Rebels-77 Clemson-75.

My name is José Valdez IV and these are my thoughts.

Notes:

- **The sweater reference is a slight one from *Three Amigos*. To this day, whenever anyone in my immediate family opens a present, they say the El Guappo line "It's a sweater!" in full Mexican accent.**

- I predicted the scores of all three of the games (La Salle, DePaul, and Clemson) at the Puerto Rico tournament and was surprisingly close on all three of them. One of the members of the Spirit Board took note of this and mentioned it in one of his posts. For his sake, I hope he didn't wager any money on future games based on my predictions.

José's Thoughts on The Eagles

José was very excited when he first heard that the Rebels would be playing The Eagles in Southaven. Not as excited as he was when Ole Miss girls finally banded together and decided that showing cleavage was appropriate for most every occasion, but still excited. *Note: José saw cleavage maybe five times in his entire Ole Miss tenure, and those were all at formals. If you went to Ole Miss in the mid 90's or later you have no idea how good you had it.*

José apologizes for the digression, but he imagines that you feel the same way José does on that matter. He must admit that he has always had great respect for The Eagles. While often being overshadowed by the competition, they have still managed to have many successful years and have delivered much joy to their fans.

That being said, José believes the current Rebel team presents significant match-up problems for The Eagles. José thinks Chris Warren will easily be able to take Don Henley off the dribble, Glenn Frey will have a hard time defending the three from Eniel Polynice, Kenny Williams should own the boards over Joe Walsh, Dwayne Curtis shouldn't have any problem posting up Don Felder, and Timothy B. Schmit will have difficulty crossing half-court against the defensive pressure of Trevor Gaskins. José must face reality here, as much as he appreciates their music, these Eagles should not be able to hang with the current version of the Rebels.

One problem José does have with The Eagles is the song "Tequila Sunrise". This is the song about the young hired hand who hooks up with his friend's lady. This is wrong on so many levels José feels he must address it. First, if you do hook up with your friend's lady, do not, under any circumstances, write a song about it. You should keep that kind of thing to yourself (trust José on this one). Also, if you make a mistake like that why would you possibly feel the need to bring tequila into it? It is not necessary to defame the reputation of a perfectly good spirit that has brought joy and happiness into the lives of José and his people. José much prefers the song "Tequila" by The Champs. It is upbeat and festive. You may remember this song as the one from the Ken Burns documentary about the young man who goes on a quest to retrieve his stolen bike. There is a poignant scene where he is about to be mauled by a biker gang after knocking over their motorcycles, but achieves redemption by performing an interpretive dance to the song.

What is that you say? The Rebels are playing the Southern Miss Golden Eagles? Well, that changes everything. There are many things José would prefer to think about rather than the Golden Eagles which include:

- Honky tonk women
- What did Coach Kennedy have for breakfast?
- Why did it take so long for Bruce Willis to figure out that nobody, other than the kid who saw dead people, was talking to him in The Sixth Sense?
- What is Coach Kennedy's favorite color?
- Whatever happened to Erik Estrada?
- Why doesn't Coach Kennedy return José's calls?

If José must think about this USM team he can say that he does not like the Eagles. One of the five worst experiences of José's life as a fan of the Rebels occurred against this team. It was the 1986 NIT match-up between the teams in Hattiesburg and there was not enough tequila on the planet to get José out of the funk he was in after that game. What made matters even worse is that José was at the game with his girlfriend. Yes, José did once have a serious girlfriend in college (in addition to the numerous ladies he had from the Niagara Falls area). *Note: José knows what you are thinking. "Since this was 1986, would you have been wearing your Miami Vice jacket to the game José?" The answer is yes, and if you think he stood out at like a sore-thumb at Ole Miss you should have seen him in his white cotton jacket among the sea of black and gold polyester that night in Hattiesburg. On the bright side, it was probably the last time José was among the majority by virtue of having his hair parted in the middle.*

Another thing José remembers about that night is later at Señor Frogs when Jorge and Paco got into a fight over which Willie Morris book was the best. Jorge insisted it was *Good Ole Boy* while Paco was adamant that

North Toward Home was the best. *Note: José stayed out of this one because he enjoyed The Courting of Marcus Dupree even more than either of those.* After much punching, kicking and some bloodshed, Jorge and Paco agreed to disagree.

José would like to see the Rebels exact some revenge for that bitter defeat and he plans to be there with José V to try to erase the memories of that night. He believes that Coach Kennedy will have the boys ready. Rebels-84 Eagles-70.

My name is José Valdez IV and these are my thoughts.

Notes:

- "Tequila Sunrise" is a depressing song. Good. But depressing.
- The Ken Burns documentary reference is about *Pee Wee's Big Adventure*.
- I made a factual error in these thoughts. The NIT game against USM was actually in 1987. That was a completely miserable experience. I couldn't even watch the second half. I kept my head in my hands and just listened to the roar every time Southern scored.
- The "numerous ladies… from the Niagara Falls area" is one of my favorite lines from *The Breakfast Club* and one I use on a regular basis.
- *The Courting of Marcus Dupree* really is my favorite Willie Morris book.

José's Thoughts on 2007

2007 was a year of ups and downs for José. Since he is not up so much on current events (only recently hearing about that whole Iran-Contra deal), José would like to share his thoughts on things that are of importance to him.

Ole Miss Football- José went into the 2007 football season with lower expectations than he has ever had for a Rebel team. These expectations were even lower than he had for New Coke, Van Halen without David Lee Roth as the lead singer, and *Weekend at Bernie's 2*. Despite having such low expectations, the Rebels failed to even meet them. By any measure, the 2007 football season was a disaster of Talmudic proportions. José could have made more productive use of his time trying to master "Through the Fire and Flames" at expert level on Guitar Hero 3, than spending it on the train wreck that was Ole Miss football this year.

However, 2007 did end on a positive note with the hiring of Coach Nutt and José feels very good about the future of the program. On the scale of excitement level for José it ranks somewhere between winning an ultimate frisbee intramural championship and Phoebe Cates showing up in Oxford to film a movie while José was in school (If you saw *Fast Times at Ridgemont High* there is really no explanation necessary).

On a personal note, José recorded his seventh documented sighting of Bigfoot in 2007. There was possibly an eighth sighting but the creature was sans cape and did not appear to be as hairy, so it is entirely possible that it was just Jorge's Aunt Ed (short for Edwina) walking through the forest searching for firewood.

Ole Miss Baseball- The 2007 baseball season was a successful one by most measures. The team did well in SEC play and advanced to yet another Super Regional. As with most fans though, José was frustrated by many late leads blown in key games (which led directly to an unhealthy increase in José's tequila consumption) and the failure to advance to Omaha. The Rebels have had three consecutive opportunities to make it to the College World Series and have been as successful as José in his first three marriages. José does fully believe that the baseball team is eventually going to make it to Omaha, just as eventually one of his relationships will survive (although he has more confidence in the Rebels).

On another personal note, 2007 was the first full-year in many that José was not married for any period of time. He has already documented the recent six-month internet relationship that ended on somewhat of a downer. *Note: If you missed that entry just think The Crying Game and you'll get the picture.* José is ready to get back on the horse though and will be evaluating candidates at various establishments throughout the mid South in 2008. Is The Dock still open? José had much success there back in the 80's. At least that is the story he is sticking to.

Ole Miss Basketball- 2007 began with a team that exceeded everyone's expectations as Coach Kennedy burst onto the college basketball scene and led his Rebels to a co-championship of the SEC West. *Note: Ole Miss is blessed with great coaches in all major sports now, but in José's opinion, Coach Kennedy is "The Big Toe".* The season ended with a second round loss in the NIT, but most Ole Miss fans saw good things on the horizon. The year now comes to a close with another team, with a great blend of youth and experience, unbeaten and ranked in the top twenty-five in the country. The excitement around this program should reach fever pitch before long.

The only downside José saw to Ole Miss basketball in 2007 was the restraining order Coach Kennedy had placed on him. Apparently José and Coach Kennedy have differing opinions as to what constitutes "stalking". Anyway, the fifty-yard buffer zone still allows José to sit on the opposite side of Tad Smith about half-way up, so it is manageable. Plus José has been able to abide by virtually every other restraining order that has been placed on him (Phoebe Cates, the Rebelettes of 1987, every Miss Mississippi from 1984-1999, and Nipsey Russell), so he has that going for him.

Unfortunately the year did end on somewhat of a down note as Jorge and Paco got into a fight at the Valdez Christmas party over which version of a classic Christmas carol was the best ever. Jorge insisted it was Bing Crosby's "White Christmas" while Paco was adamant that Gene Autry's "Rudolph the Red Nosed Reindeer" was superior. *Note: Jose stayed out of that one because he knew that Nat King Cole's "The Christmas Song" was unquestionably the best ever.* After some punching, kicking, and a little bloodshed, Jorge and Paco agreed to disagree.

My name is José Valdez IV and these are my thoughts.

Notes:

- Were it not for the hiring of Coach Nutt late in the year and the fast start by the basketball team, 2007 might have been the most depressing year in my life as an Ole Miss fan.

- Unfortunately I never saw Phoebe Cates around town while she was filming *Heart of Dixie*. I did run into Ally Sheedy though in the Kroger parking lot.

- There are four other movies referenced in this one: *Fast Times at Ridgemont High*, *Raising Arizona* (Aunt Ed), *Stripes* and *The Crying Game*.

- I actually had no success with women at The Dock that I can recall.

- The Nipsey Russell mention comes because I had a dream not that long ago that I met him. Possibly the strangest appearance in any of my dreams.

- Nat King Cole's "The Christmas Song" is the best Christmas Carol ever and I will fight anyone who says differently.

José's Thoughts on Alabama A&M

Alabama A&M University is located in Normal, Alabama, which is just outside of Huntsville. Huntsville is the home of the Redstone Arsenal and NASA Marshall Space Flight Center. "What is the significance of this José?" you ask. This is where they built the Saturn V rockets that were used to pretend to take men to the moon. José has previously stated the reasons why it is impossible for men to land on the moon, but if you need to see how it was accomplished, José recommends you see the movie *Capricorn One. Note: O.J. Simpson plays one of the astronauts so you know it is credible.* Also, it is interesting to note that Werner Von Braun and his team of German scientists worked at the Redstone Arsenal and developed the rockets. These are the same people who had a hand in the Germans bombing of Pearl Harbor.

Let José clearly state that although he has not fallen into the trap that many of you have by believing that man actually landed on the moon, he certainly does believe in UFO's and aliens. "But José," you say. "I thought the only legends you believed in were Bigfoot and El Chupacabra?" That is true, but aliens do not fall into the legend category. There is well documented proof all over the internet of their existence. If you think there was a cover-up concerning Area 51, you cannot imagine what occurred in areas 29, 33, and 47.

José must admit that he has not given much thought to Alabama A&M over the years, since there has not been much reason to think about them. Truth be told, there are many things José would prefer to be thinking about early in 2008 which include:

- Where can José find a 2008 Jessica Alba calendar?
- What will it take to keep Coach Kennedy happy at Ole Miss?

- Were any of the old Colonel Reb mascots tempted to just put on the head and go streaking down Sorority Row? *Note: José would have been.*

- Does Coach Kennedy own a Tivo and if so, what does he have on season pass?

- Whatever happened to Kelly LeBrock?

- What is exactly is a $#$&$%^$? *Note: This is what Coach Kennedy called José the last time he called the Coach's home.*

José's challenge before every game is to find something that he dislikes about the Rebel's opponent. In most instances, especially in games against SEC teams, it is not difficult. Initially, José thought it would be difficult to find the necessary motivation for disliking this Alabama A&M team. There are plenty of things José does not like about the state of Alabama. These include: the University of Alabama, Auburn University, the speed trap in Wilmer, Alabama fans, Auburn fans, the girl from Montgomery who caused José to miss the famous Doug Flutie hail-mary play, the Alabama coach, and the Auburn coach. But, José shouldn't hold all of that against Alabama A&M.

On the surface, there would appear to be nothing to dislike about this Alabama A&M team. The school is the home of John Stallworth, the great Pittsburgh Steeler receiver. *Note: In José's opinion Stallworth was better than his much-heralded teammate, Lynn Swann.* However, when José learned that Alabama A&M's mascot is the Bulldogs, and their colors are maroon and white, that changed everything.

For the life of him, José cannot understand why any school would want to pattern themselves after The School Whose Name Shall Not be Spoken. This seems to fall into the category of bad ideas along with the time José decided that Wife #2 wouldn't mind if he missed their anniversary to go to Las Vegas with Jorge and Paco (Hence the need for Wife #3). That trip is also memorable because it was the time Jorge and Paco got into a fight over who was the better world news anchor, Dan Rather or Tom Brokaw. Jorge insisted it was Rather while Paco was adamant that Brokaw was superior. *Note: José wasn't crazy about either of them, but sided with Paco. Still, he kept his mouth shut. Jorge is a biter.* After many punches, kicks and some bloodshed, Jorge and Paco agreed to disagree.

The Alabama A&M team comes in with a 3-6 record. Their last game was an 11-point loss to Auburn. José thinks that Coach Kennedy has the boys ready to play in their last game before SEC play begins. Rebels-97 Bulldogs-65.

My name is José Valdez IV and these are my thoughts.

Notes:

- The reference about putting on the Colonel Reb mascot head and going streaking is in honor of my friend and college roommate, Sam Hubbard, who was Colonel Reb for two years in the late 80's. John Robinson, William Foushee (his other roommates) and I often threatened to do this while Sam was out. There was a strict rule that no one else was supposed to put on the head, but we often sat on the couch and watched tv while wearing it just to make him mad.

- I (along with most of the people I know) have received a speeding ticket in Wilmer, Alabama.

- There really was a girl who caused me to miss the famous Doug Flutie play. I'm still bitter about that, but she wasn't from Montgomery.

José's Thoughts on Tennessee

José must turn his thoughts to the University of Tennessee and the biggest game of the season to date. The excitement José feels can be rivaled only by the rush he got when José III threw him into the Rio Bravo (you Gringos call it the Rio Grande) when José was a child and told him to start swimming. *Note: This was also the occasion for José's first use of profanity. Lest anyone out there think that he condones this, José would like to stress to the children out there to refrain from using profanity. You adults can have at it.*

José can say without hesitation that he does not like Tennessee, the University or much anything else about the state. His thoughts regarding all things Tennessee are as follows:

- Orange is not as cool a color as Red. (Especially on chicks).
- Tennessee Pride doesn't taste as good as Jimmy Dean (JD's sausage rocked José's world).
- Tennessee Williams was an inferior writer to William Faulkner.
- "Rocky Top" is not in the same league as "Dixie".
- Tennessee Ernie Ford wasn't as great as Johnny Horton
- Estes Kefauver paled in comparison to John Stennis.
- The Tennessee River has much less water than the Mississippi.
- Tennessee Walking Horses aren't as impressive as Clydesdales.
- Saturn vehicles are not as nice as Nissan ones.
- Peyton Manning is not as loved by Archie and Olivia as Eli is. (You know this. José knows this. The American people know this.)

- Jack Daniels is not quite on par with Jim Beam. *Note: José doesn't really believe this last one but he had to stick with the theme. Please keep the Jack Daniels coming Tennessee. José cannot survive on tequila alone.*

Another problem José has with Tennessee is that someone once tried to look under a bathroom stall at him on campus in Knoxville. *Note: Perhaps José should have refrained from sharing that disturbing bit of information, but his "counselor" told him he should be more transparent.* Looking back, this may have been Senator Larry Craig on a visit to the state. Also, José dislikes Tennessee so much that he would not even consider a woman from there for wife #4 (unless she was very good looking, did not require extensive laser hair-removal, and had no more than one extra appendage. José has high standards).

The coach of Tennessee is Bruce Pearl. José does not like him either. You may recall that Pearl showed up at a Lady Vols game last year, shirtless, painted orange, and wearing a headband. José recalls his first shot of tequila as well. Honestly, José does not want to see that kind of thing. In fact, he does not want to see any coaches doing such a thing. However, these coaches top José's list of those he does not ever want to see shirtless and painted any color of the rainbow: Rick Majerus, Charlie Weiss, Ralph Friedgen, and Mark Mangino. José may need a shot of tequila right now to get these images out of his head. He has found in the past that it worked with certain disturbing things such as:

- The scene in *Deliverance.*
- Accidentally seeing Aunt Edna naked.
- The breakup of Journey
- The entire movie *Seven.*
- The "leave Brittney alone" dude on YouTube.
- The whole Exxon Valdez incident. (Why couldn't it have been the Exxon Rodriguez?)

As for the game, José expects it to be a knock-down, drag-out fight. Much like the time Jorge and Paco got into a fight over who was hotter, Salma Hayek or Catherine Zeta-Jones. Jorge insisted it was Salma while Paco was adamant that CZT was better looking. *Note: Normally José stays out of these frays but he felt obligated to punch Paco in the eye on this occasion.*

Anyway, José expects Coach Kennedy to have the boys ready to play. Rebels-74 Inferior Sausage Making Vols-71.

My name is José Valdez IV and these are my thoughts.

Notes:

- The reference to Jimmy Dean sausages rocking his world comes from a comedian doing an impression of Harry Carey.

- That bathroom stall incident at UT really happened. I won't go into any more detail. That happened the year the SEC Basketball Tournament was in Knoxville. The other thing about that tournament I remember is that my roommate, Sam Hubbard, was in his Colonel Reb suit practicing trick shots before the game and he hit one of the shot clocks, breaking it. He may be the only mascot in history to delay the start of a basketball game.

- Does anyone not think Archie and Olivia are fonder of Eli because he went to Ole Miss?

José's Thoughts on LSU with Special Commentary from José III

Louisiana State University in Baton Rouge is the flagship school of the Louisiana State University system. This sounds impressive until one recognizes that it is the approximate equivalent of saying that Vanilli was the more talented half of the pop duo Milli Vanilli.

In José's opinion there are two kinds of people in the world; those who think *Raising Arizona* is one of the funniest movies ever made and those who don't appreciate that kind of humor. José is in the former category while most LSU fans would fall into the latter. José believes this is quite possibly because so many Tiger fans are like the characters in the movie and don't get the joke. In fact they could have easily picked up the trailer, taken it out of the Arizona desert, placed it in the bayou and called it *Raising Louisiana*. José is almost certain he saw Gail and Evel Snoates painted purple at the LSU football game this past Fall.

While we are on the subject of movies, and by "we" José means Jorge, Paco, Paco's retrievers Anthony Michael Hall and Ally Sheedy (don't ask), and himself, José must confess that he has always been bitter about the movie *Everybody's All-American*. The film was based on the book by Frank DeFord and in the movie version the hero was an LSU football player. When José was in school the rumor was that there were talks to film the movie in Oxford and have the hero be an Ole Miss football star, but the administration would not approve of having it filmed here because of some disagreeable aspects of the story. José believes this to be accurate because he got it from the same source who told him that the Mikey kid from the Life Cereal commercials died while drinking Coke and eating Pop Rocks.

José made some comments in an earlier offering concerning being tired of having to listen to José III talk about the glory years and how many games the Rebels lost while he was in school. Well José III took exception to this and requested that his voice be heard. The true and actual thoughts of José Valdez III are as follows:

"Comes Jose Valdez III to demand some space from his wayward son Jose Valdez IV. Jose Valdez III thought he had taught the boy better than to make snide remarks about the Glory Years under

Coach Vaught, which Jose Valdez III did indeed enjoy immensely. Bear with the old man as he relates one of his best Ole Miss football memories. First, the stage must be set. Everyone remembers what happened in Red Stick Halloween night 1959. Jose Valdez Jr. and Jose Valdez III suffered through that when Trey was a mere senior in high school. It's funny how most people forget what happened January 1, 1960 and that the 1959 Rebels were named the SEC team of the decade; they gave up a total of 21 points. The 1960 Rebs tied the LSU kittens during Homecoming on the Ole Miss campus as an injured Jake Gibbs limped onto the field to lead a last-minute drive for the tying field goal. Jose Valdez III was a freshman. The great 1961 Rebel team lost to LSU in Red Stick 10-7. Can anyone forget the picture in the annual of the gallant quarterback Doug Elmore exiting the field with his beautiful girlfriend and tears in his eyes? Jose Valdez III was a sophomore. Then came 1962 when Jose Valdez III was a junior and the Rebs had to play the kittens in Red Stick again. Yes, 3 out of 4 years in the kittens' lair, and 2 losses and one tie to show for the past three games! Jose Valdez III made sure he showed up in Red Stick to help right the ship. Golden Arm Glenn Griffin led the Rebels with his throwing and his legs to a 15 – 7 victory in the kittens' packed den. The silence of the LSU crowd at the game's end was one of the sweetest sounds Jose Valdez III never heard! The Rebels proceeded to complete their first undefeated and untied season and to win their 5th SEC championship. How sweet it was!!!"

José IV must admit that he has had some nice moments being a fan of Ole Miss, but none that rival those of José's II and III. They got to enjoy greatness while José IV has enjoyed a lifetime of "building character". He would very much like to begin witnessing some greatness soon though and while excited about the future of the football team, believes that the highest level of excellence is coming sooner from Coach Kennedy and the boys.

This LSU basketball team is bad, possibly the worst to come to Tad Smith in José's memory. José will not be shedding any tears for them though. With the Rebels coming off of their first loss of the season, Coach

Kennedy is mad. He is probably angrier than he gets when José stands at the edge of the court-ordered 50-yard buffer zone with a bullhorn and sings "You Can Do Magic" to him.

Coach Kennedy will have as much mercy on LSU as Rocky had on Clubber Lang in the rematch. Rebels-82 Tigers-54.

My name is José Valdez IV and these are my thoughts.

Notes:

- I really did hear that about *Everybody's All American* wanting to film in Oxford, but not being given permission. I don't know if it's true or not but I believed it.

- Surely everyone is aware of the Mikey – Pop Rocks story.

- The José III comments are from my Dad, Jim Crockett, who is a serious author. He has written *Operation Pretense* and *Hands in the Till*. He's currently working on his third book. He understands about one-tenth of my references because he watches a movie about once every five years.

- Of course after making the comment about the LSU team being so bad, they came close to beating the Rebels and actually did defeat them later in the year in Baton Rouge. I'll keep those thoughts to myself in the future.

José's Thoughts on Florida

Some people say that José doesn't know a boatload of crap about Ole Miss basketball, but he does. He knows this team is special, will be playing very meaningful games come March, and that José, Jorge, and Paco will be taking their show on the road to follow the team.

Also, José does not want to hear that Coach Kennedy is "one of the best young coaches" in America. He is not even "the best young coach in America". He is "The best coach in America" period and José will fight anyone who says differently. *Note: He will also fight anyone who: questions the authenticity of his Bigfoot sightings, makes snide comments about him parting his hair in the middle, is Lithuanian, a carnie, a Lithuanian carnie, or who doesn't think that Mr. Tom Petty is the most handsome man alive.*

José has had a difficult time turning his thoughts to the Florida game since the close-call victory over LSU. There have been many things on his mind including:

- Does Coach Kennedy like stromboli's from Pizza Den?

- Is that really Tim Tebow's girlfriend's picture all over the internet? (If so, José salutes you Mr. Tebow)

- Does Coach Kennedy regret the mullet-hair days as much as José does?

- Are there ten people out there who really understand what the hell is going on in the first 100 pages of Faulkner's *The Sound and the Fury?*

- Will Coach Kennedy hunt José down like a dog for the mullet comment?

We must now turn our thoughts to Florida. The state is perhaps best known for being the home of the band 38 Special. José has many memories of cruising for chicks unsuccessfully in his El Camino listening to "Rockin' Into the Night" and "If I'd Been the One". Back in the day 38 Special was like the American version of Menudo, except they played instruments and didn't suck. José also likes the beaches, the theme parks, and the ladies of the Sunshine State. José remembers a Spring Break in Destin where the beer flowed like tequila. He also recalls going to Nighttown one evening when they had the incredible "Ladies Drink Free" promotion. This was the idea that you offer free drinks to females in the hopes that they will try out your establishment and guys will show up to see all of them, spending a lot of money in the process. Brilliant! However, do not make the mistake of assuming this strategy will work for any type of business. For example, if you were to own a Krispy Kreme donut franchise, you would not want to run a "Ladies Eat Free" promotion or you'd end up with a bunch of "plus-sized" women from The School Whose Name Shall Not Be Spoken" eating you out of business.

But José digresses. He realizes that he may be in the minority, but José has always liked the Florida Gators and has no trouble pulling for them in any sport when they aren't playing the Rebels. José even liked Steve Spurrier when he was there. *Note: For José readers under the age of five, Spurrier has not always been the coach of South Carolina.* Spurrier made José laugh, especially when he teased Phil Fulmer by saying you can't spell "Citrus" without "T-E-N-N-E-S-S-E-E".

Wait a second. That makes no sense whatsoever. José must have told it wrong. Anyway, Phil Fulmer is fat. Steve Spurrier made fun of him. José liked it.

The Gator basketball team is the two-time defending national champions. Their coach is Billy Donovan, who may be the second best coach in America. You may or may not recall that he left Florida during the off-season to become the coach of the Orlando Magic. He remained in this position for five days before returning to the Gators. This was less than the amount of time José spent recently in the Oxford Jail. *Note: José firmly maintains that he was racially profiled in this incident and that had he been Caucasian and parted his hair on the side he would never have been detained for camping out in Coach Kennedy's backyard.*

While we are on the subject of the Florida Gators, José must confess something. He lied to many of you recently and is ashamed to admit it. If you were in the crowd for the Ole Miss-Florida game this past season then José offers his sincere apology. Before the game, on the minitron, when everyone was asked "Are you ready?" José answered in the affirmative, when in fact he was not ready. It had been a difficult drive to Oxford. The family truckster had suffered a flat tire. José V and little Josélina had been grumpy and José did not feel very good about the Rebels chances that afternoon. He should not have done what he did, but alas, José is just a man. If you prick José, does he not bleed? If you tickle José, does he not laugh? If you place tequila in front of José, does he not drink? Anyway, he promises to be more honest about his feelings going forward and will most certainly be ready come tip-off time against the Gators.

The Florida football game was also the occasion for the fight between Jorge and Paco over who was closer to being right, the Baptists or the Methodists. Jorge insisted it was the Baptists while Paco was adamant that the Methodists were correct. *Note: José stayed out of this one since he is Presbyterian.* After many punches, kicks and some bloodshed, Jorge and Paco agreed to disagree.

The Florida game is a huge one for the Rebel basketball squad. José expects it to be close the entire way, but Coach Kennedy will have his boys ready for everything. Rebels-82 Gators-80.

My name is José Valdez IV and these are my thoughts.

Notes:

- The "doesn't know a boatload of crap" reference comes from the movie *Nacho Libre*. I think my kids have watched it one-hundred times.

- The reference to Mr. Tom Petty being the most handsome man alive is something the character Lowell once said on the television show *Wings*.

- This one included my second reference to strombolis from Pizza Den. The best sandwich ever made. I still get one on just about every trip to Oxford.

- As it turns out, those pictures were not of Tim Tebow's girlfriend. Just a very impressive young lady who happened to get a picture taken with him.

- I really didn't understand the first one hundred pages of *The Sound and the Fury* for quite some time. My plan was to try again every five years until I got it. I think I was finally able to make some sense of it when I was thirty.

- I do know Spurrier actually said you can't spell Citrus without UT.

- The family truckster reference is from *Vacation*.
- The "if you prick José" portion is inspired by Shakespeare's *The Merchant of Venice*.
- I really am Presbyterian. That becomes clear in later thoughts.

José's Thoughts on Auburn

José does not enjoy spending time thinking about Auburn University. There are numerous things he would rather think about, which include:

- Does Coach Kennedy know about In-N-Out Burger?
- Which "clothing optional" resort is closest to Pontotoc?
- Does Coach Kennedy have a MySpace page?
- If Willie Morris were alive today would he be writing *The Courting of DeAndre Brown?*
- Would Coach Kennedy consider lessening the distance limitation in the restraining order against José from 50 yards to 25?

Unfortunately, José must turn his thoughts to Auburn, which apparently has grocery stores made of solid gold and if you're an athlete, Sociology is the major of choice. One of José's fondest memories is being present at Jordan-Hare Stadium to witness the Rebel football team defeat Auburn in their first match-up against The Coach Whose Name Shall Not be Spoken. If you were watching on television, perhaps you saw José acting like a drunken Mexican (which he was not, at least the drunken part) in the stands after the Auburn 4th down pass fell incomplete in overtime. It was certainly one of the top five Ole Miss sports memories for José. Incidentally, that was the first time José had been on television since a late 80's road trip with Jorge and Paco through the Midwest found them at a Cubs-Pirates game one afternoon. As the camera panned the crowd in the outfield bleachers, the great Cub announcer Harry Caray exclaimed, "Heeeeyyyyyyyy! Check out the guy in the sombrero!" That was José in his finest hour. Chicks dig sombreros. *Note: Should you happen to locate a copy of the game in question, this occurs just after Harry says, "Bobby Bonilla spelled backwards is Ybbob Allinob."*

As previously stated, Auburn is the home of The Coach Whose Name Shall Not be Spoken. That is reason enough for José to hold them in disdain. If there is one thing José is known for it is his ability to maintain a grudge (Ok. Perhaps he is better known for his tequila consumption, parting his hair in the middle, failed marriages and internet relationships or his collection of *Land of the Lost* action figures, but José really can hold a grudge). In earlier offerings he has also made reference to The School Whose Name Shall Not be Spoken, and The Wife Whose Name Shall Not be Spoken. José has not however, shared the laundry list he has of others who have offended him and Whose Names Shall Not be Spoken from his lips. These include, but are not limited to:

- The Prom Date Whose Name Shall Not be Spoken
- The Proctologist Whose Name Shall Not be Spoken
- The Time/Life Operator Whose Name Shall Not be Spoken
- The Tech Support Guy Whose Name Shall Not be Spoken
- The German Shepherd Whose Name Shall Not be Spoken
- The 8th grade Algebra Teacher Whose Name Shall Not be Spoken
- The Former Lead Singer of Van Halen Whose Name Shall Not be Spoken
- The Career Counselor Whose Name Shall Not be Spoken
- The Former Ambassador to Uzbekistan Whose Name Shall Not Be Spoken

José feels better for having gotten that off of his chest. Not as good as he felt when Jerry Lawler got his sweet revenge against Wildfire Tommy Rich after Rich cost him his hair match against Austin Idol, but still pretty good.

José neglected to mention that his great Auburn football game memory was marred only by the fight Jorge and Paco got into over which U2 song was the best. Jorge insisted it was "Pride" while Paco was adamant that "Bad" was superior. *Note: For 20 years José would have agreed with Jorge, as he claimed that "Pride" was his all-time favorite song, but he recently came to the realization that "Bad" is actually better and that he'd been living a lie all of this time.* After many punches, kicks, and some bloodshed, Jorge and Paco agreed to disagree.

If the Ole Miss basketball team is going to have the kind of year so many expect, it is critical that they win a few SEC road games. This one would appear to be one that is theirs for the taking. José does not expect it to be easy. However, he does expect Coach Kennedy to have the boys ready to play. Chris Warren has a big game. Rebels-82 Tigers-75.

My name is José Valdez IV and these are my thoughts.

Notes:

- **In-N-Out Burger is fantastic. Unfortunately they are only out West. If you have a chance go, and get a double-double. Ask for it animal style with the grilled onions.**

- **The reference to Sociology being the major of choice at Auburn was because of the academic scandal that involved the football team and certain courses in that department.**

- **I was at the '99 Auburn game. I was not at a Cubs game in a sombrero.**

- **Regarding my *Land of the Lost* reference, someone posted something negative (which I have no problem with) about this particular offering on one of the message boards. I recall that another poster told that person they had the "sense of humor of a Sleestak." I thought that was pretty funny.**

- **I really did not like my 8th grade algebra teacher. He didn't like me either.**

- **That Jerry Lawler-Tommy Rich incident was available on YouTube last I checked. It's classic stuff.**

- **I do think *Bad* is the best U2 song.**

José's Thoughts on the School Whose Name Shall Not be Spoken

José knows what you are thinking. You are wondering which Emily Dickinson poem best captures José's feelings after the Auburn game. He must go to Miss Dickinson's "An Awful Tempest Mashed the Air" to describe the depth of his depression.

> *An awful tempest mashed the air,*
> *The clouds were gaunt and few;*
> *A black, as of a spectre's cloak,*
> *Hid heaven and earth from view.*

José recognizes that the same poem probably was on many Rebel fans minds after the crushing loss to the Tigers. He also must admit that it has been a long time since José was as despondent as he was after that game. In fact, the last time he can recall being that chagrined was when the International Astronomical Union revoked Pluto's planetary status. *Note: José hopes that you will join him in protesting this grossly unfair decision by discontinuing financial support for the IAU. They will not get one more peso from José! He is officially redirecting his financial contributions to The Human Fund.*

Well the Auburn game is in the past and there is no use crying oneself to sleep in tequila soaked sheets any longer. José must turn his thoughts to The School Whose Name Shall Not be Spoken (or TSWNSNBS for the purposes of this offering). José finds it very amusing how fans of TSWNSNBS obsess over Ole Miss (much the same way José obsesses over Salma Hayek, Coach Kennedy, Bigfoot and chicken chimichangas).

The level of obsession became apparent to José after their football team defeated the Rebels in 2005. Despite the fact that they finished the season with a less-than-glamorous 3-8 record, they had t-shirts printed that read "2005 Egg Bowl Champions". *Note: Maybe José should have had History Bee 11th place t-shirts printed for himself since he finished ahead of Jorge (and only Jorge) in the 8th grade at Santa Poco Academy. (Paco finished one spot ahead of José because he knew that the Mexican General defeated by Sam Houston at the Battle of San Jacinto was Santa Anna and not El Guapo).*

José must also address that he has had difficulty gathering his thoughts because of the terrible smell that is permeating his room. You see he accidentally stepped into some maroon earlier in the day.

Honestly, José cannot get over the decision to use "Step Into the Maroon" as the promotional campaign for TSWNSNBS. However, it does make more sense after hearing the other options that were considered. They included:

- "Consistently delivering average to below results since 1878."

- "You can always go somewhere else for graduate school."

- "The best education you can get in the Golden Triangle area or my name ain't Doc Foglesong!"

- "What other options do you have?"

- "Come to school here and your odds of getting a job are 10% higher than those with only their GED."

- "Exactly how high are your expectations anyway?"

- "Only 24 Rhodes Scholars and 3 Miss Americas fewer than Ole Miss!"

- "Just pay your fees and you can tell people you went to school anywhere you'd like."

- "Don't believe everything you hear."

- "University of Memphis turned you down? We're still here."

One of José's very favorite things to do is to approach fans of TSWNSNBS who happen to have teenage daughters and tell them that their daughters just might be good looking enough to go to Ole Miss. They typically respond with a weak laugh as if José is joking with them, but José gets the sense that they are not really amused. But let us be honest, probably 75% of all TSWNSNBS grads either secretly wish they had gone to Ole Miss or hope that their children do. Of course you could never get them to admit to this, but you and José both know it to be true. Now try to think of ANY Ole Miss grad who might secretly wish they had gone to TSWNSNBS. That didn't take long. It would be like José wishing his perfectly coiffed hair (circa Patrick Swayze 1990) looked more like Jorge's comb-over.

As for the game, José recognizes that this is an extremely important contest and is doing his part to encourage Coach Kennedy. Last night José stood outside Coach Kennedy's window with a portable stereo held over his head playing "In Your Eyes". Fortunately for José, he escaped before the cops arrived.

Expect the Rebels to play with reckless abandon, much the way José approached ultimate frisbee, road trips, and nights at The Gin when he was in school. Rebels-76 TSWNSNBS-72.

My name is José Valdez IV and these are my thoughts.

Notes:

- **The Human Fund reference comes from the charity George Costanza invented on *Seinfeld*.**

- **Santa Poco was the village in the movie *Three Amigos*.**

- **The 2005 Egg Bowl Champion t-shirts really did kill me.**

- **I don't even know any State fans who thought "Step into the Maroon" was a good idea.**

- **It's now 25 fewer Rhodes Scholars than Ole Miss.**

- **The "In Your Eyes" bit is in reference to John Cusack doing the same thing in the movie *Say Anything*.**

José's Thoughts on the Super Bowl

José must reveal something that may be disturbing to many of you. (Do not be alarmed though, this has nothing to do with the time José put on the Colonel Reb head and went streaking down Sorority Row). What José must reveal is that he likes the Patriots. He really, really likes the Patriots. (*Note: José will not go so far as to say that he loves the Patriots as love is such a strong word that he reserves it for the Rebels, Salma Hayek, tequila, and "Welcome Back Kotter"*).

Virtually every Rebel child of José's generation was a Saints fan for the obvious reason that Archie Manning was the quarterback. Most boys had posters of Archie on their walls (along with Farrah Fawcett and Kiss posters ... unless one's mother was Southern Baptist). But what many today may not understand is that there was an unwritten rule among boys that being a Saints fan automatically qualified one to have an "alternate" favorite team; a team that might actually have a chance to win a championship. Many, including Jorge, rooted for Roger Staubach and the Cowboys. Others like Paco, were Steelers fans. José, never one to go along with the crowd (unless the crowd was headed to a Styx concert), went with the Patriots of Steve Grogan, John Hannah, Russ Francis, and Sam "Bam" Cunningham and has remained a fan to this day.

Now y'all without sin can cast the first stone.

Please bear with José. It is as difficult for him to admit that he is a Patriots fan as it was for him to reveal to his career counselor that his true desire is to be a lion-tamer. But he really is a Patriots fan. José is crappin you negative.

José can certainly understand some of the hatred for his Patriots though. Belichick is about as likeable as The Wife Whose Name Shall Not be Spoken. They have had a lot of success and most people would like to see another team experience the thrill of winning a Super Bowl. Jealousy just goes with the territory. José can relate here as he experienced the same type of reaction in his Miami Vice jacket wearing days (which lasted an additional four years after the show was cancelled).

So José finds himself in the awkward position of seeing his 18-0 Patriots, going for immortality, playing against one of Ole Miss's favorite sons, and the player who took the Rebels their greatest success in José's life as an Ole Miss fan, Eli Manning. What is José to do?

He must say that the choice is even more difficult than when he had to decide whether to take twelve hours in a semester and actually graduate or just take six and finish up in the Spring so he could hang around for Gerald Glass's final basketball season (José chose the latter).

Ultimately it comes down to José's affection for all things Ole Miss. Even though sometimes it seems Ole Miss doesn't return the love to José (just like Salma and Coach Kennedy), he cannot turn against a great Rebel.

Go Giants!

My name is José Valdez IV and these are my thoughts.

Notes:

- I was definitely concerned about getting some negative feedback once I revealed I was a Patriot's fan. I suppose mentioning that I was for the Giants in the game prevented this. Pulling for the Pats does go back to the 70's for me, but I also ended up living in Foxboro for a little while. My son Wes was born while we lived there. Ironically, my older son Will had an Eli Manning Fathead poster on his wall, while Wes had Tom Brady. They both pulled for the Giants in the game though.

- I did not have a Farrah Fawcett or Kiss poster on my wall. My mother is Southern Baptist.

- The "Now y'all without sin can cast the first stone" line is from *Raising Arizona*.

- The reference to wanting to be a lion-tamer is from a Monty Python sketch.

- The "crappin you negative" line is also from *Raising Arizona*.

- I did own a Miami Vice jacket, but I grew up in Pensacola so cut me some slack.

- **I did indeed take six hours each semester my final year of graduate school so I wouldn't miss Gerald Glass's senior season.**

José's Thoughts on Vanderbilt

José knows what you are thinking. You are wondering which REO Speedwagon song best expresses José's state of mind after the debacle last Saturday. His answer might surprise you. Indeed he was despondent after the crushing loss. In fact the last time he can recall being that down was when, despite his best efforts, using all of his charm and unleashing some of his best pick-up lines, he was unable to garner any interest from either of the Indigo Girls after their concert in the Grove when José was in school. He still has trouble figuring out exactly what went wrong. Anyway, José is past that, and the game, and turns to REO Speedwagon's song "Ridin' the Storm Out" to summarize his current attitude.

> Ridin' the storm out, waitin for the thaw out
> On a full moon night in the Rocky Mountain Winter
> My wine bottle's low, watchin for the snow
> I've been thinking lately of what I'm missing in the city

The Rebels and José will ride this storm out. It may end up being like his all-time favorite Disney World attraction, Mr. Toad's Wild Ride (which has since been replaced by some freakin' Winnie the Pooh deal). There will be ups and downs, twists and turns, laughter and terror, but in the end it will bring satisfaction to Ole Miss fans.

Before he moves on to Vanderbilt, let José offer you some advice. Do not, under any circumstances, wait for the team bus to arrive back in Oxford after a loss, holding a sign that says "Don't give up Coach Kennedy. Was it over when the Germans bombed Pearl Harbor?" José made the mistake of doing so and was abruptly pelted with rocks and garbage. Just give Coach Kennedy some space and let him cool off for a while. Lest you think this was the first bad idea José has ever had, rest assured, it was not. It does belong among an elite group of bad ideas he has had though, which include going to a formal with the Crazy Phi Mu Whose Name Shall Not be Spoken and paying money to see the movie *Ernest Goes to Camp*.

Vanderbilt University was founded in 1873 and named for Cornelius Vanderbilt, the shipping and rail magnate, who provided the initial $1 million endowment. Surprisingly, Vanderbilt gave the money despite having never been to the South. José has no problem with this as he regularly provides funds to save the lemurs, yet has never visited Madagascar.

José really doesn't have anything against Vanderbilt University. In fact he strongly considered matriculating there, but on his campus visit he discovered that both of the good-looking girls who attended Vandy were already in serious relationships. *Note: José would like to dispel the notion that the fact that his SAT score was 500 points below the average Vanderbilt freshman played any part whatsoever in his decision.*

This is a critical game for both Vanderbilt and the Rebels. With both coming in at 2-3 in the SEC, a loss would virtually end all hopes of a division title. Expect both teams to play with heart and passion. José does not want to even think about the possibility of losing this game, just as he doesn't want to think about what a world without David Hasslehoff might be like.

José can recall some painful losses to Vanderbilt in different sports. The OT football loss in David Cutcliffe's second game with the Rebels comes to mind. Last year's defeat in the SEC Baseball tournament was especially frustrating as well. That was the time Jorge and Paco got into a fight over which was the better tv show theme song; the one from *Baretta* or for *Magnum P.I. Note: José stayed out of this one because although he thought both were great, he preferred the theme song to Hawaii Five-O to either of them.* After much punching, kicking, and some bloodshed, Jorge and Paco agreed to disagree.

Coach Kennedy and the boys are about to begin a long stretch of better play. Rebels-83 Commodores-77.

My name is José Valdez IV and these are my thoughts.

Notes:

- **This includes the second mention of Disney World discontinuing Mr. Toad's Wild Ride. Can you tell I'm bitter?**

- The "pelted with rocks and garbage" is from a very old David Letterman show where he tried to start a new catch phrase. "They pelted us with rocks and garbage" was one of the choices. I believe it lost out to "What do you want? Wicker?" which I still say on occasion.

- I did go to formal with a crazy person one time, but she was not a Phi Mu.

- I did not pay money to see *Ernest Goes to Camp*.

- I think my comment about Vanderbilt only having two good looking girls offended one of our Ole Miss message board readers who happened to have two daughters there. Maybe they were the two I saw.

José's Thoughts on South Carolina

José regrets that his offerings may become less frequent going forward. You see he was contacted yesterday by a member of the Nigerian royal family who is looking to come to America. He needs to transfer all of his funds to an American account immediately and of all the people he could have chosen to help him, he selected José. All José had to do was provide him with his bank account numbers so he could arrange the transfers. Once he arrives in America, the gentleman will open his own account but will give José $1 million for his trouble. In other words José is about to be rich. Since he will be living a life of luxury (drinking only the newest wine), José probably will not be inclined to spend as much time penning his thoughts.

For now though, José will share his thoughts. José must admit that he typically does not spend much time thinking about South Carolina. In fact there have been many things on his mind lately other than the Gamecocks, which include:

- Does Coach Kennedy believe in UFO's?
- How much tequila is too much tequila?
- Has Coach Kennedy seen *Die Hard*? (It was awesome).
- Why can't there be some kind of alumni Derby Day where former Ole Miss sorority girls come back and do the dances? *Note: José feels it is inappropriate for a 40-something year-old Mexican to hide in a tree so he can watch college students at Derby Day. He still does it, but it is inappropriate.*

- Why did Coach Kennedy return the sweater José sent him for Christmas?

The University of South Carolina is perhaps best known for being the home of Hootie and the Blowfish. Although none of them graduated, all four members of the band attended the school. If you have never seen Hootie in concert you might be able to catch them along with Right Said Fred and Glass Tiger at a Ramada Inn lounge or County Fair in your area soon.

On to Gamecock athletics. José is certain everyone was already aware that the University of South Carolina is the three-time defending Women's Hunt Seat Equestrian National Champions. José would like to congratulate the Fighting Lady Gamecock Horsy Riders on defeating the other two schools that compete in this particular sport.

Actually José has witnessed an athletic contest at the University of South Carolina. He was there to see the Rebels defeat the Gamecocks in football when they were in the midst of their twenty-something game losing streak. José must admit that he was impressed by the fan support of such a terrible team. José recognizes he should probably be a more supportive person. Had he been such a person José might still be with Wife #1, and could have completely avoided Wife #2 (The Wife Whose Name Shall Not be Spoken) and Wife #3 (who vamoosed with José's life-sized wax-sculpture of Coolidge from The White Shadow).

Even though José enjoyed seeing the Rebels defeat the Gamecocks in football that evening, he won't be going back. That happened to be the night Jorge and Paco got into one of their worst fights. This one was over who was the greater English poet, Shelley or Keats. Jorge insisted it was Shelley while Paco was adamant that Keats was superior. *Note: José agreed with Paco on this one, believing "Ode to a Nightingale" was greater than anything Shelley wrote. But he stayed out of it. Jorge is a biter.* Because the fight turned into a barroom brawl, (who knew South Carolinians had such strong opinions on English literature?) Jorge and Paco were arrested for the disturbance they caused and were taken to the local jail. Fortunately, after spending the weekend there they managed to escape (or as they like to put it "released themselves on their own recognizance."). Do not worry about them being tracked down and caught though, they's usin' code names.

José believes that Coach Kennedy has the boys prepared for a good stretch of basketball. Rebels-75 Gamecocks-60.

My name is José Valdez IV and these are my thoughts.

Notes:

- The "drinking only the newest wine" is a reference from the movie *The Jerk*.

- The *Die Hard* reference is from *The Chris Farley Show* skit on *Saturday Night Live*. Man I miss Chris Farley.

- If they ever do decide to hold some sort of alumni Derby Day I'd pay good money to see a few women get knocked into a mud pit.

- I loved one of the responses I got to this selection. It read, "Don't hate on Hootie." It is ironic that the former lead singer, Darius Rucker, recently had the #1 song on the country music charts. I don't suppose he'll be appearing at a Ramada Inn anytime soon.

- The "released themselves on their own recognizance" and "they's usin' code names" are both lines from *Raising Arizona*.

José's Thoughts on Arkansas

As many of you surmised, the Nigerian "royal family" deal turned out to be a scam. Not only did José not receive his $1 million, but his checking and savings accounts were completely depleted. When José visited his local bank to tell them of his predicament, he was informed that he may be the first person under ninety-seven years old to fall for that particular scam. It was also suggested to José that someone "that gall dern stupid" should not be allowed to handle money. Anyway, José is now on the market for a job so if any of you boys are looking for a smithy or someone otherwise trained in the metallurgic arts, José is your man.

Unfortunately, José is generally a trusting person. This has come back to haunt him on many occasions, most notably when Wife #3 vamoosed with his DVD boxed set of season three of "BJ and the Bear". José must chalk the entire episode up as another lesson learned though. He adds it to his growing list that includes, but is not limited to:

- When the road sign says "One Way", the Texas Highway Patrol prefers you go in the direction the arrow is pointed.

- Do not exceed the recommended dosage of Viagra (especially within five hours of a job interview).

- Baptists frown on bringing malt liquor to dinner on the grounds.

- "Sex Panther" cologne does not achieve the desired results

- Coach Kennedy hates Mexicans (at least ones who sing "Every Rose Has its Thorn" outside his office window after a loss).

José must admit that he finds it difficult to take the state of Arkansas seriously. Although it became a state in 1836 it was forty-five years later before it was finally agreed upon how the name should be pronounced. Apparently many in the state said "Ar-Kansas" while others said "Arkan-Saw". In 1881 the state legislature officially declared that the latter was the correct pronunciation. Perhaps José should not be so hard on Arkansas as he once, in the heat of passion, accidentally mispronounced Wife #1's name of "Consuela" as "Guadalupe" (hence the necessity for Wife #2).

In José's opinion, Mississippi is better than Arkansas in every way. He turns to the great Brazilian poet Antonio Goncalves Dias to summarize his feelings of the Magnolia state's superiority to its neighbor to the northwest:

> *Our heavens have more stars,*
> *Our meadows far more blooms,*
> *Our forests have more life,*
> *Our life has much more love.*

José apologizes for the digression but he felt the need to Brazilian Wax poetic for a brief moment.

On to the University of Arkansas. As many of you were already aware, a team of University of Arkansas engineering students won the 2006 world championship for solar powered boats. It was a rigorous competition, which captivated the attention of scores of people in the Fayetteville/Russellville area, but in the end, the boat created by these Arkansas students did prove to be superior to the entry from Madison-Ridgeland Academy's eighth grade science team.

Concerning the game against Arkansas this Saturday, José must admit that he has had difficulty getting mentally prepared for it after the devastating loss last Saturday. José has not been that down since Ruth and Jimmies served its last plate lunch. But the Rebels and José must persevere. They must persevere like the wind.

José expects a courageous effort from Coach Kennedy and the boys. Rebels-82 Solar Powered Boat Champions-80.

My Name is José Valdez IV and these are my thoughts.

Notes:

- **"That gall dern stupid" is another *Raising Arizona* line.**

- "Smithy or someone otherwise trained in the metallurgic arts" is from *O Brother, Where Art Thou?*

- The reference to the Texas Highway Patrol preferring you go in the correct direction on a one-way street is from a time I was riding with my friend Sam Hubbard in Mesquite, Texas. The highway patrolman pulled us over, and after looking at Sam's driver's license said, "Son, I don't know how you boys do it in Mississippi, but here in Texas, when the sign says one way, that's the direction we go." Sam got off with just a warning.

- The "Sex Panther cologne" reference is from the movie *Anchorman*.

- "Persevere like the wind" was inspired by "sew like the wind" from *Three Amigos*.

José's Thoughts on Presbyterian

José knows what you are thinking. You are wondering which Grand Funk Railroad song best captures his state of mind after the loss last Saturday. His answer might surprise you. No, things have not gone as well as José expected lately, but he is still optimistic. The toughest part of the schedule is behind the Rebels and he looks for no worse than a 6-2 finish in the remaining SEC games. The GFR song "Shinin' On" best expresses his current attitude:

> *We are winners and losers, bed fellow choosers*
> *Put here to pass by the times.*
> *We are space-age sailors, all had our failures,*
> *Now everybody gonna' shine.*

José understands that many fans have lost faith and now believe the team is not going to reach the heights they were certain of earlier in the year. José would rather light a candle than curse your darkness.

But José digresses. It is time to focus on the Presbyterians. They are coming to Oxford and they are not happy, especially considering that they currently sport a 4-22 record. The four victories have come against Simpson Academy, The Washington School, Jackson Academy (in double overtime) and Magnolia Heights. The Presbyterians haven't been this dispirited since the Penal Laws in Ireland banned them from public office in 1707. Being Calvinists, José would expect the Presbyterians to recognize that they are predestined to lose to the Rebels, and lose badly.

Presbyterian College has one of the more interesting nicknames in all of collegiate athletics. *Note: Not as interesting as the Stormy Petrels of Oglethorpe University. José loves that name.* Presbyterian College is the Blue

Hose, though José is not certain what kind of hose is referred to here. Is it a garden hose or fire hose? Perhaps it is denotes an air hose or radiator hose?

What is that you are saying to José? It refers to stockings?

Well that's just dumb.

Anyway, José is certain you were already aware that the largest bronze statue of a Scotsman in the entire world can be found on the campus of Presbyterian College. What less than half of you probably knew though, was that José is in possession of the seventh largest statue of a Scotsman, along with the fourth largest wood carving of William Shatner.

"I didn't know José was a Star Trek fan," you say.

In fact José is not a trekkie. He was, however, treasurer of the Central Mississippi T.J. Hooker fan club. José believes there are two kinds of people in the world; those who love William Shatner, and those who recognize they are unworthy to speak his name.

Concerning the actual game, José has come to the realization that Presbyterians really should not play basketball. He knows this because he is a Presbyterian. Sure, they make fine bankers, physicians, attorneys, and bean field workers, but basketball players they are not. Quick, name five great Presbyterian basketball players. You cannot do it. You cannot name one. In Genesis, God told Abraham that he would spare the city of Sodom if he could find ten righteous men. The resulting destruction of the city would have been just as certain if God had told Abraham to produce one decent Presbyterian basketball player. Show José a good Presbyterian basketball player and he'll show you a closet Seventh-Day Adventist.

As proof, José offers you:

- Michael Jordan- not a Presbyterian.

- Wilt Chamberlain- not a Presbyterian.

- Larry Bird- not a Presbyterian.

- Oscar Robertson- not a Presbyterian.

- Jimmy Chitwood- not a Presbyterian.

Since religion has found its way into this offering, José would be remiss if he did not mention that one of Jorge and Paco's worst fights ever was over the proper mode of baptism. Jorge is Methodist, so adheres to sprinkling. Paco is Baptist and insists that dunking is biblical. José stayed out of that fight because although he is Presbyterian, he is not completely convinced of the correct procedure. In fact, José has been sprinkled, dunked and also ran through the sprinkler at his cousin Jefe's to make sure he had all of his bases covered.

Rebels-147 Blue Panty Hose wearing Calvinists-55.

My name is José Valdez IV and these are my thoughts.

Notes:

- I was off on my prediction of a 6-2 finish to the SEC regular season. The Rebels finished 4-4 and that cost them an NCAA bid.

- The "would rather light a candle than curse your darkness" is yet another line from *Raising Arizona*.

- Regarding my assertion that Presbyterians could not play basketball, my friend Bob Mims, who did not know I was the person writing these, sent a message to my inbox listing a few decent Presbyterian basketball players, but then admitted that there weren't any really good ones.

- With my admission of being a Presbyterian and a victory over Jackson Academy being mentioned in these thoughts, one poster made the assumption that I must have gone to Jackson Prep. I actually went to public school in Pensacola, Florida. My three children go to Jackson Academy.

- My comments concerning baptism sparked a bit of a religious dialogue on one of the message boards. Some people apparently took me way too seriously on this one.

José's Thoughts on Alabama

So José was slightly off on his prediction of the margin of victory the Rebels would have over the Blue Panty Hose wearing Calvinists (by 81 points). He advises you against giving anything he says too much credence. As he is often reminded, José has made the following statements:

- "Boy that Dukakis will be hard to beat."

- "Whitney Houston and Bobby Brown sure make a great couple."

- "Yes, Peyton Manning is good, but how can you pass up Ryan Leaf?"

- "They can never make enough Police Academy movies."

- "Go for it Jorge. I'm positive that's a chick."

- "Surely the replay official will get it right."

José does feel a little better after the Rebels defeat of the Presbyterians, but not a whole lot. Winning that game seemed to be as certain as finding José at the gym or the gun club on a Friday afternoon. Yes, José is very manly and does mostly manly things.

José must acknowledge that he has alternated least favorite SEC teams over the years (other than The Team Whose Name Shall Not be Spoken. They are in their own category). When Peyton went to Tennessee they became his least favorite. After The Coach Whose Name Shall Not be Spoken went to Auburn, they moved into that spot. However, with the addition of Nick Saban and the Doyle Jackson incident, Alabama currently occupies José's most hated school status. He hates them more than he hates Wife #3 (who vamoosed with José's autographed photograph of Morgan Fairchild).

Because he is still upset about the football game this past year, José has decided he is boycotting all things Alabama. Since there is a Mercedes plant in Tuscaloosa County, José will not be purchasing one of their vehicles. He will just have to see if the El Camino can hold out another five years. Because Jim Nabors is an Alabama grad, José will not be watching any Andy Griffith episodes featuring Gomer Pyle. (José could not realistically be expected to give up the show entirely). Finally, José will no longer be attending races at Talladega. *Note: In fact, José has attended only one race there, but it was not a pleasant experience. He is aware that NASCAR is huge, that it appeals to fans from all walks of life (José's brother Diego is a huge fan) and one need not be a redneck to appreciate the sport. However, none of the fans José sat amongst appeared to have gotten that memo. Rarely has José been more out of place than he was in the stands at Talladega Motor Speedway. He felt like the Lost Mohican.*

Speaking of Doyle Jackson, the Alabama football game this past season was the scene of a particularly violent fight between Jorge and Paco over which is the most underrated Charles Dickens novel. Jorge insisted it was *Nicholas Nickleby*, while Paco was adamant that *The Old Curiosity Shop* was the most underrated. *Note: José stayed out of that one because he believes Barnaby Rudge is actually Dicken's most underrated offering.* After many punches, kicks, and some bloodshed, Jorge and Paco agreed to disagree.

The game against Alabama is incredibly important. The Rebels have four remaining opportunities to obtain a road victory and likely need to win at least two of them. Unfortunately the Rebels have had less luck on the road than José had on the hayride in 9th grade with Carmelita Benitez. But José did not let that get him down and he came back strong just five years later.

Tonight would appear to be one of the better opportunities to steal one though. Expect to see an especially intense Andy Kennedy and an inspired Ole Miss basketball squad. Rebels-73 Bama-69.

My name is José Valdez IV and these are my thoughts.

Notes:

- **The "gym or the gun club" reference is from *Mr. Mom*. I use it often with my wife.**

- **I actually have not been to a NASCAR race. My brother Craig is a big fan though.**

- "The Lost Mohican" is actually from a fantastic quote by former Yankee centerfielder, Mickey Rivers, who once said, "Man, the wind must have been blowing 100 degrees out there. I felt like the Lost Mohican." Priceless.

- I am a big Dickens fan, thanks to a course I took under Natalie Schroeder at Ole Miss. All of the books I listed are underrated.

- This game was my one road game to attend on the year. It was incredibly frustrating.

José's Thoughts on Auburn Chapter Dos

And then depression set in.

There are many possible explanations for the recent slide the Rebel basketball team has experienced. Perhaps relying on so much youth and inexperience is finally catching up with the team. Maybe enjoying tremendous offensive success early on kept the boys from developing the defensive mental toughness they would need to succeed in conference play. It's quite possible that the fans had unrealistic expectations after the quick start and the standard was set too high.

Those are all plausible explanations for what has transpired lately, but José believes he has finally realized what the issue truly is.

Jesus hates José.

There can be no other rational explanation why José's dreams are continually crushed beyond recognition. Jesus just will not allow José's favorite team to enjoy the success he so greatly desires. José cannot understand why he has been singled out for condemnation when there are plenty of other sinners (some even worse than José) supporting different schools from around the country.

Oh, the signs were there all along, José is just now beginning to understand their significance. Perhaps the El Chupacabra shaped birthmark should have alerted José to the fact that there was a problem. But lots of people have those, right? When he was a young boy, José's mother Margherita (May she rest in peace) sang "Jesus Loves Me" to José's brother Diego every evening when she tucked him in. She sang "Ring of Fire" to José. That probably should have tipped him off as well.

Alas, José cannot continue to wallow in self-pity (although he is very good at wallowing). He must turn his thoughts to Auburn. One thing that has always bothered José about Auburn is the plethora of nicknames they have. They are called the Tigers, Plainsman, and some people even assume they are the War Eagles. *Note: War Eagle is technically one of their cheers and not a nickname, but they do fly an Eagle into the stadium before football games. This seems about as logical to José as the Rebels having a meerkat race onto the field during the pre-game Hotty Toddy.* Actually José should probably be a little more understanding about the abundance of nicknames Auburn has, since he has many nicknames his damnself (There José goes. Sinning again). They include, but are not limited to:

- The sensitive naked guy. (From his college days).

- El Diablo de Santa Poco. (His mother called José this).

- The Gangster of Love (The moniker José gave himself. It hasn't caught on).

- *%!&!P *#*&%! (What Coach Kennedy calls José).

- Looser. (What Jorge, Paco and the population at large call José). *Note: José always thought the correct spelling was L-O-S-E-R, but perhaps his English is not so good. Thus, he defers to the generally accepted message board spelling of the word.*

There is one positive thing about Auburn that José must acknowledge. Former Rebel football great George Plasketes is a member of the faculty in the Department of Communication & Journalism. Plasketes was a childhood hero of José's and was a defensive end on the 1977 team that defeated Notre Dame. For those too young to remember, Plasketes also worked the PA system for Ole Miss baseball games while he was in school and was friggin' (technically not a cuss word) hilarious. He is famous for asking all of the School Whose Name Shall Not be Spoken Rhodes Scholars to line up along the first baseline one afternoon. His other spiel was to say, "Here are some scores from around the SEC… 4 to 2, 6 to 3, 7-1, 5-0, and a partial score…8." Come home George Plasketes.

Needless to say, the Rebels must win the game against Auburn this Saturday. José does not want to even entertain the possibility of a loss. Just as he does not want to entertain the possibility that Pablo Cruise may never release another album. Although his confidence is shaken, José predicts the Coach Kennedy's boys will emerge victorious. Rebels-11 Auburn-9. And in honor of the great George Plasketes, José offers you his predictions on the other SEC games this Saturday. 81-76, 64-63, 77-59, 68-57, and a partial score 55.

My name is José Valdez IV and these are my thoughts.

Notes:

- The "El Chupacabra shaped birthmark" was inspired by a song by The Barenaked Ladies, but they mention a pentagram shaped one.
- My mother is actually still alive and is not pleased that I killed her off in my José thoughts.
- The Sensitive Naked Guy was a skit on Saturday Night Live.
- The "Gangster of Love" reference is from the Steve Miller Band song.
- I really hesitated putting the reference to spelling the word "loser" incorrectly, but I couldn't resist because it, or just the word "lose", is so often misspelled on the boards. Fortunately I didn't catch any flack for it, and some people found it amusing.
- I got to meet George Plasketes a few years ago while on campus at Auburn. He was a fantastic guy.
- The Rebels did end up losing this game and it was probably the most costly loss of the season.

José's Thoughts on The School Whose Name Shall Not be Spoken Chapter Dos

Well, it happens like clockwork every February. The Sports Illustrated swimsuit issue comes out and within a week the cover model has some sort of frivolous "stalking" charges pressed against José. In his defense, who among us has not seen the swimsuit issue, immediately gotten on a plane to fly halfway around the world, and followed the cover model's every move for the next three days while singing Night Ranger's "Sister Christian" into a megaphone?

But José digresses. He must examine the subject at hand; the current state of Ole Miss Basketball. It doesn't take a rocket surgeon to figure out that something is terribly wrong with this team. The collapse that is currently happening rivals those of the Ptolemaic Dynasty, the Roman Empire, and Van Halen. José would have never believed this possible a few weeks ago, but then again José was also shocked to see *Balls of Fury* shut out when the Oscar nominations were announced.

There are only seven remaining regular season games to turn this thing around and it all begins with a very tough opponent. A victory over them might give the Rebels the confidence they need to make a run and finish strong.

The School Whose Name Shall Not be Spoken (or TSWNSNBS for the purposes of this offering) is approximately 125 miles northeast of Jackson, 23 miles west of Columbus, and for all intents and purposes, 1,000,000 miles from Oxford and Ole Miss. They can create their own version of The Grove, try to build a square, but they can never be what they most desire to be. Actually, José can somewhat sympathize with TSWNSNBS and their inferiority complex, because for many years his greatest wish was that he could be a ladies man on the level of Antonio Banderas. Recently though he recognized that was never going to happen and José set his sights much lower; to be a ladies man more on par with Cheech Marin. José suggests that the TSWNSNBS and Starkville redirect their efforts to something that might possibly be attainable as well, such as being more like Arkansas State and Jonesboro. It would take some effort, but with the proper vision and leadership, it could happen in the next ten years.

As everyone who knows José can attest, he is essentially an amiable person. He is human however and must admit to certain things he finds disagreeable:

- Bad tequila - Fortunately for José he has rarely come across bad tequila.

- Poems that do not rhyme - José's stuff doesn't rhyme either, but then he doesn't claim to be a poet.

- Wives #2 and #3 - Wife #1 was actually ok and José would take her back tomorrow but for the tasering incident.

- Neptune - By far the most overrated planet.

- Bryant Gumbel - José would rather listen to Gilbert Gottfried announce a game than Gumbel.

- Body doubles - If you're advertising Jessica Alba, then José wants friggin' Jessica Alba.

- The Liver - José much prefers the Pancreas, which despite secreting important digestive enzymes and producing hormones, never gets the glory that the Liver gets.

- TSWNSNBS - José is not alone here as God-fearing people all over the country feel the same way. Apparently Ellis Johnson does as well.

While he is on the subject of TSWNSNBS, José must admit to something that may shock some Rebel fans, especially younger ones. There was a time when he enjoyed listening to Jack Cristil on the radio. This was back in the late 70's/early 80's when Cristil was only about seventy-five years old. It was actually cool to hear Cristil say the name "Kalpatrick Wells", not as cool as hearing Stan Torgerson say, "Stroud shoots. Heeeeeee

Scooooorrrrrrreesssss!!!!", but still pretty cool. These days Cristil sounds as though he is suffering from permanent hemorrhoids and his head could explode at any moment.

Speaking of the late 70's/early 80's, José would be remiss if he didn't mention the great New Year's Eve fight of 1979 between Jorge and Paco over which was the better band; Earth, Wind & Fire or The Commodores. Jorge insisted it was EWF while Paco was adamant that the Commodores were superior. *Note: While José considers both to be outstanding, it just doesn't get any better than Maurice White, Phillip Bailey and the Earth, Wind & Fire gang. However, he kept his mouth shut. Paco is an eye-gouger.* After many punches, kicks and some bloodshed, Jorge and Paco agreed to disagree.

Hopefully Coach Kennedy and the boys will be ready to play Wednesday night. José has not done so well with his predictions lately so he is going to try the reverse hopper approach this time and see what kind of results he gets. TSWNSNBS-99 Rebels-40.

My name is José Valdez IV and these are my thoughts.

Notes:

- **Bryant Gumbel has since been relieved of his NFL announcing duties to the great relief of every person I know.**

- **The pancreas reference comes from a comedy bit I heard long ago where a guy sang "Let us all raise our glasses to the pancreas."**

- **This post gave me away with someone. I previously mentioned that Bob Mims commented on the Presbyterian article. By mentioning Earth, Wind & Fire in this one, after writing the Presbyterian one, he figured out I was the one writing José because he knew I was a fan. This should not have happened because I had originally written this one with a reference to Tupac Shakir's "Keep Ya Head Up", but the day I planned to post this I read "The Sports Guy" on ESPN.com and he was using the same song in his article. I had to delete that reference because I didn't figure anyone would believe I had written mine first. I substituted the EWF/Commodores reference instead.**

José's Thoughts on Minnesota

Before moving on to the mighty Golden Gophers of Minnesota, José must address last night's basketball game. While he would like to think that using the reverse hopper approach in his prognostication had some sort of impact, the reality is that the coaches and players deserve all the credit. The team came out with a lot of intensity from the opening tap and while you typically hear of a team feeding off of the energy of the crowd, last night José felt the crowd fed off the energy of the team. It has been many years since José has seen a Tad Smith (not Tad Pad) crowd into the game from start to finish like it was last night. The night was so good that Jorge and Paco exchanged no punches, kicks, or bites, only an awkward man-hug. All that being said about the coaches and team deserving all the credit, expect José to employ the reverse hopper approach for the remainder of the basketball season.

And now it is time for Ole Miss Baseball. No one is more pleased about this than José. He doesn't want to go into all the details, but José will say the last time he was this excited involved a honky-tonk woman, the Benbow Village hot tub, some tequila, and Atlantic Starr playing on the portable stereo. You know what José is talking about. Don't pretend that you don't.

José is a sports fan. He loves football, both college and professional. There are few things more exciting than being in the crowd for a big college basketball game like last night. But baseball is José's passion. He looks forward to sharing many thoughts on Ole Miss Baseball this season and hopes that his final ones of 2008 will be written from Omaha.

We must turn our thoughts to Minnesota.

"What do we need to know about Minnesota?" you ask.

Well there are many interesting things about the state of Minnesota that everyone should be aware of. Most important is that MacGyver is from there. How cool is that? If Dan Tanna were from Minnesota it might be the second best state in the country, but alas, he is from Ohio. You should be interested to know that the Coen brothers and Vince Vaughn are Minnesotans. Musically the state can boast of Bob Dylan, Prince, and The Replacements. The state has given the world the literary genius of F. Scott Fitzgerald and Sinclair Lewis. Finally, were you aware that 91% of Minnesotans own health insurance? That is the highest percentage in the country. José salutes you Minnesota.

José has actually visited the fine state of Minnesota. He took Wife #1 (pre-tasering incident) to the final two games of the 1991 World Series between the Twins and Braves. José came into a little money (He bet on Redd Foxx in his Dead Pool) and decided he would do something he had never had the opportunity to do before, and might never have the chance to again. It was an amazing experience, seeing two of the great World Series games ever. The list of things that stand out from the trip includes:

- Minnesota is freakin' cold. José drank hot tequila the entire time.

- If Lonnie Smith picks up where the ball is on his way to second base in the 8th inning of game seven, he scores and the Braves are World Champions.

- Trying to put this as nicely as possible…the women of Minnesota are…not very attractive.

- The pitching duel between Jack Morris and John Smoltz in game seven was as good as it gets.

- There are a whole lot of white people in Minnesota.

As for the University of Minnesota, the school lists more official songs than any school José has ever come across. They include "Minnesota Rouser", "Minnesota March", "Go Gopher Victory", "Our Minnesota", "Minnesota Fight", "Hail! Minnesota", and "The Battle Hymn of the Republic". José is astounded they have not added "Purple Rain", "Raspberry Beret", and "When Doves Cry" to their compilation.

José is certain everyone was already aware that Loni Anderson is a graduate of the University of Minnesota, but you may not have known that the great Mexican singer, Lila Downs, is also an alumnus. Miss Downs performed in the Oscar nominated song "Burn it Blue" from the movie Frida, which starred the goddess Salma Hayek. Salma made a few appearances sans clothing in the movie which more than made up for the fact that she sported a uni-brow for the duration of the film.

The University of Minnesota is one of the largest schools in the country and has about 17,000 more female students than Ole Miss (though approximately 8,000 fewer good-looking ones). If you doubt this, José suggests you visit the Twin Cities and see for yourself as José did. Loni Anderson may be the last babe Minnesota has produced and she's sixty-one.

This weekend provides an opportunity for the Rebels to somewhat avenge one of the great injustices in college football history. The 1960 football season saw a 10-0-1 Rebel team finish second in the AP poll to a clearly inferior 8-2 Minnesota team. Back in those days (when José III was at Ole Miss) the final polls were voted on prior to the bowl games. Minnesota, which had been behind the Rebels in the polls, with their one loss, heading into the final week of the season, was voted the national champions in the final poll and then proceeded to lose the Rose Bowl to Washington 17-7. José III is still not happy about that and in many childhood beatings José received, the subject was mentioned, though it seemed to have no relevance whatsoever to the situation at hand.

A Minnesota basketball team, led by Kevin McHale, also knocked the Rebels out of the NIT in the early 80's. That was a particularly bad night as it was also the time Jorge and Paco got into a fight over who was the best looking Charlie's Angel. Jorge insisted it was Farrah Fawcett, while Paco was adamant that Jaclyn Smith was superior. *Note: While José found them both gorgeous, he was loyal to the third angel, Kate Jackson, because she was a Rebel.* After many punches, kicks, and some bloodshed, Jorge and Paco agreed to disagree.

As for the baseball games this weekend, José believes Coach Bianco has the boys ready for a fast start. He will not employ the reverse hopper approach with the baseball team until necessary. Rebs over Gophers 6-2, 7-4, 9-1. And so the march to Omaha begins.

My name is José Valdez IV and these are my thoughts.

Notes:
- **I did indeed live at Benbow Village for a couple of years. There were some good responses to the hot tub reference.**
- **I did take my wife to the last two games of the 1991 World Series and it was amazing.**

- There were quite a few people who refuted my assertion that Minnesota women were not very attractive. Apparently some of the Ole Miss fans who travelled there for the baseball games the year before were quite impressed with the local talent. I say they were imported.

- My Dad is still upset about that 1960 National Championship deal.

José's Thoughts on LSU Chapter Dos

Go to hell LSU!

My name is José Valdez IV and these are my thoughts.

Notes:

- **Possibly my all-time most popular thoughts.**

José's Thoughts on Northwestern State

If the Minnesota series is any indication, this could be the baseball season José has been waiting for his entire life. Of course José has been waiting for Gil Gerard to send the autographed picture he requested for approximately the same amount of time, so there are no guarantees.

Before José begins his thoughts on Northwestern State he feels he has no choice but to address the rumor currently circulating that he once made out with a certain Miss Mississippi while he was in school. While José can neither confirm nor deny this rumor, he encourages each of you to ask five friends if they have heard it, and for those five to inquire with five others, and so on and so forth.

Northwestern State University is located in Natchitoches, Louisiana. Natchitoches is actually pronounced "Nak-i-dish" which makes about as much sense as pronouncing "José" as "Günter". If you have ever visited Natchitoches, as José has, you are well aware that they are quite proud of the fact that Steel Magnolias was filmed there. If you are a dude and have ever seen Steel Magnolias, just keep that to yourself. José does not need to know that about you.

José would be remiss if he did not at least reference the fact that Ed Orgeron is a graduate of Northwestern State. However he sees no need to delve into the subject any further. José has moved on from the Orgeron experience just as he moved on from Wife #3 (who vamoosed with José's entire Aldo Nova record collection). It took some time, but José eventually realized that he and Wife #3 were just a fool's paradise.

José earlier mentioned a trip to Natchitoches. He must admit that it is a beautiful town, but when he visited, the hotel accommodations were somewhat lacking. He stayed at a Holiday Inn, which may have been the only hotel in America where there were no other buildings within sight. That was not the most interesting thing about the visit though. When José checked in there were ladies everywhere. You would think he would have been in heaven, being that he was single at the time. Unfortunately, these were not Ole Miss sorority girls José is talking about. It didn't take long to discover the "Welcome Lady Bass Anglers" banner hanging in the lobby and realize what was going on.

Before someone takes umbrage with José, he does not mean to insinuate that there are not some fine looking ladies who fish. He is certain that many of you have wives, girlfriends, mistresses, etc. who like to drop a line now and then, and are fine looking women. However, José sincerely doubts that any of your wives, girlfriends, mistresses, etc. were present in Natchitoches that particular week. In fact, José probably has never had a lesser chance of picking up (unless you count the Miami Vice wearing jacket years of 1986-92) than he had on that stay.

The Demons of Northwestern State come to town with a first year head coach. He is Jon Paul Davis and although he was named the head coach last August, the NSU baseball website still lists him as the pitching coach next to his picture in the coaches section, which may not be a good sign. José will also say that from looking at the picture, Coach Davis is dangerously close to parting his hair in the middle. He will need to make the part more definitive, comb it differently (bangs are a necessity) and wait one year, since he is only thirty-four, before he can join José's exclusive club though. Even then, there is no guarantee that Tom Petty or Mark Richt won't blackball him.

It will be interesting to see how the Rebel mid-week pitchers perform against Northwestern State. José expects that they will answer the bell and get the job done. Rebels 8-4, 12-3.

My name is José Valdez IV and these are my thoughts.

Notes:

- **For those unfamiliar with Gil Gerard, he was the star of *Buck Rogers in the 21st Century*. Hey, we only had four channels when I was a kid.**

- **The first of my *Steel Magnolias* references. The ultimate chick-flick.**

- "Just a fool's paradise" is yet another *Raising Arizona* reference. You have probably surmised by now it is my favorite comedy.
- The Lady Bass Anglers story really happened to me in 1991.

José's Thoughts on Kentucky

José knows what you are thinking. You are wondering which Merle Haggard song best expresses his feelings after the LSU debacle. Since Merle had so many good ones it is not an easy decision. José could go with "I Think I'll Just Stay Here and Drink", but instead he chooses "Everybody Gets the Blues" to describe his despair.

> Everybody's had the blues sometimes and
> Everybody knows the tune.
> And everybody knows the way I'm feelin cause
> Everybody's had the blues.

Hopefully after the Kentucky game Merle's "Natural High" will be on José's mind.

José must turn his thoughts to the Wildcats.

You were probably already aware that the state of Kentucky is the home of the two largest man-made lakes east of the Mississippi. You may not have been aware that José owns the two largest velvet Elvis's east of the Mississippi, but west of the Tennessee- Tombigbee.

Of course one cannot think of Kentucky Basketball without thinking about Ashley Judd. The movie starlet seems to be everywhere the team plays, screaming and bouncing (you know what José is talking about) supporting her team with wild enthusiasm. She has had an interesting movie career, having appeared in some pretty good movies; *A Time to Kill*, *Heat*, and *Simon Birch*. She has also been in some bad ones; *High Crimes* and *Divine Secrets of the Ya Ya Sisterhood* (not that José saw that one). More interesting though are the relationships she has had over the years. Although currently married to the Indy Car drive, Dario

Franchitti, Judd has dated Brady Anderson, Lyle Lovett, Matthew McConaughey, Robert De Niro and most impressively, Michael Bolton. In addition to being the Barry Manilow of the 90's, Bolton sported one of the better mullets in history. (Coach Kennedy's late 80's mullet paled in comparison). *Note: If José turns up missing any time soon, you know who to question.*

Considering the attention Kentucky Basketball receives because of Ashley Judd, José has decided that Ole Miss needs to step up their efforts of building an international fan base. Rebel Marketing has done a fine job enlisting celebrities to do the Hotty Toddy at football games, but only Ole Miss fans and their opponents of the week get to see those. Shepard Smith does nice work as well, promoting Ole Miss every chance he gets, but not everyone watches Fox News. José would like to offer his suggestions on getting the Ole Miss message out and bringing in a larger fan base.

- Oprah gives out Ole Miss Grove platters to all her audience members at the special Christmas show.

- While saving the Minority Whip from being either kidnapped, shot, or blown up, Jack Bauer wears an Ole Miss sweater vest throughout this year's season of "24".

- The cast of "Lost" is rescued from the island by a plane sent by Dickie Scruggs. (Wait. Perhaps we should hold off on that one for a while).

- A former Ole Miss quarterback leads his team to one of the great upsets in Super Bowl history while earning the MVP award. (Check)

While on the subject of Kentucky, José would be remiss if he did not mention the fight between Jorge and Paco over which was the best side item at Kentucky Fried Chicken, the mashed potatoes or the slaw? Jorge was adamant that the mashed potatoes were the best while Paco insisted that the slaw was superior. *Note: José stayed out of that one, preferring the biscuits to either.*

Coach Kennedy and the boys are running out of time to salvage what was once such a promising season. Once again, José will employ the reverse hopper method of prognostication. Kentucky-106 Rebels-49.

My name is José Valdez IV and these are my thoughts.

Notes:

- I did get a Velvet Elvis as a wedding present. I think my wife sold it at a garage sale.
- I have not seen *Divine Secrets of the Ya Ya Sisterhood* and have no intention of ever doing so.
- Coach Kennedy really did have a pretty good mullet in the 1980's as I recall.

José's Thoughts on Indiana State

One of the most important things José does before any Ole Miss athletic contest is summon the proper amount of animosity for the Rebel's opponent. This is typically easy to do, especially when the opponent is The School Whose Name Shall Not be Spoken, LSU, Auburn, Alabama, etc. Unfortunately, this weekend the Ole Miss baseball team faces Indiana State and José is having a great deal of difficulty finding the motivation necessary to hate the Sycamores. After all, what is there not to like about the state of Indiana and Indiana State University? For example:

- Larry Bird is from Indiana State. Who doesn't like Larry Bird?

- Sunny Haven Recreation Park, "One of the finest and friendliest nudist parks in the Midwest" is located just outside of South Bend. *Note: For those of you making summer vacation plans, Sunny Haven is not "clothing optional" so prepare to be very nude during your entire stay.*

- Dana, Indiana native, Bert Shepard, was the only person to play major league baseball with an artificial limb. (Possibly more impressive than the one-armed drummer from Def Leppard).

- Steve McQueen was from Indiana. Name five people cooler than him. You cannot do it.

- Indiana State's mascot is the Sycamores. José is pro-trees.

The worst thing José can come up with about the state of Indiana is that the 23rd President of the United States, Benjamin Harrison, was from there. Not that Harrison was a particularly bad fellow; just that he was boring (we're talking Millard Fillmore level boring). If the crowning achievement of your presidency is that the first Pan-American Congress met during your administration, then you aren't going to have your face on a piece of currency anytime soon.

On to Indiana State University. A well known, and might José say, fine tradition at the school is "The Walk". This is an exercise in which a very large number of students, sometimes in the hundreds, walk down Wabash Avenue towards the football stadium, stopping at each bar along the way to have a beer. Being that there are approximately fifteen establishments that serve alcohol along this stretch, one can imagine the condition of the participants upon the completion of their journey. José had a similar tradition early in his college career, which primarily involved walking from The Warehouse downstairs to Forrester's, over to The Gin, across to The Hoka for a hot fudge brownie, and then back up to The Warehouse where he would start the process all over again (though on the second go-round he typically substituted potato logs at the Chevron station for the hot fudge brownie at The Hoka).

As for the series, the baseball team is off to an impressive start and José expects another strong performance this weekend. A sweep might garner them the #1 ranking in the land. Rebs over Trees 8-2, 10-3, 14-4.

My name is José Valdez IV and these are my thoughts.

Notes:

- **The "very nude" line is from the underrated Mike Myers movie *So I Married an Axe Murderer*.**

- **I did eat many a hot fudge brownie at The Hoka and potato log at Chevron back in the day.**

José's Thoughts on Alabama Chapter Dos

Being that it is Saturday and José has shared thoughts on three other Rebel opponents this week, he will keep this brief.

There are certain things José believes very strongly. These include:

- At this very moment Wife #2 (The Wife Whose Name Shall Not be Spoken) is making some poor guy's life completely miserable.

- Willie Morris was the only person ever who could make you feel like you missed out by not growing up in Yazoo City, Mississippi.

- The children are our future.

- Someday Doyle Jackson is going to Hell and he will not have to wait in line when he gets there.

Against his better judgment José is not employing the reverse hopper approach today. Rebels-77 Bama-65.

My name is José Valdez IV and these are my thoughts.

Notes:
- **My goal to this point had been to write something on every opponent no matter what the major men's sport. I came to the realization around this time that I couldn't continue at**

this pace. Trying to write four thoughts in one week was too taxing.

- The "children are our future" comment was straight from the song, but I was thinking about the Eddie Murphy version in *Coming to America* when I wrote this.

- The Doyle Jackson comment was over the top. But I really, really dislike that guy.

José's Thoughts on the NIT

José will be the first to admit that he has been negligent in sharing his thoughts lately. You probably expect him to offer some lame excuse, such as he has been working on a covert CIA operation in Kathmandu, but he is not going to do that. José is not in the CIA. He used to be. Long time ago. Doesn't like to talk about it.

José also chooses not to address the rumor currently circulating that his silence is in any way related to some sort of incarceration. However, if you would mention that you heard this to any attractive women between the ages of 25-40 who cannot resist the "bad boy" type, he would be most appreciative.

Concerning the Ole Miss Basketball season, as he is sure is the case with many of you; José couldn't help but be reminded of The Epic of Gilgamesh. Everything was rolling along just fine until Gilgamesh and Enkido had the incidents with the Bull of Heaven and Humbaba, and the gods finally decided someone had to pay. Someone involved with Ole Miss apparently offended the college basketball gods this year and José would like to know who that person is (unless it was José).

Against his better judgment José violated his own cardinal rule of being an Ole Miss fan this basketball season. The rule is a very simple one. Go into every Rebel athletic contest expecting to lose.

"That is a terrible attitude and no way to go through life José!" you say.

José does not disagree with you, but hear him out. This is not something that applies to every aspect of his life. José has no control over the outcome of Ole Miss athletic contests. Things he does have some control over, José expects to win. For example, this Summer José, Jorge, Paco, and Paco's cousin Sheldon will get together for the 15th annual

Tenzing Norgay games. This is the weekend when they drink tequila and compete in miniature golf, bowling, Texas Hold 'Em, Pictionary, and Greco-Roman Wrestling. José has trained furiously this past year and fully believes that he will take home the trophy (a ceramic Yak), despite the fact Sheldon is the twelve-time defending champion.

José admires those Rebel fans that are eternal optimists and would never encourage them to change. In fact, he discourages you from doing so. José has just found that this approach keeps him from hurling ferrets off of bridges. However, he is not going to pump sunshine up your skirt and tell you its raining. Let José be clear that he is not committed to this approach forever. Just give him one SEC football championship, Final Four, or College World Series appearance and he promises to change his outlook.

The Rebels face the University of California-Santa Barbara in the opening round of the NIT. UCSB is perhaps best known as the alma mater of Lon McEachern, host of ESPN's World Series of Poker. The Gauchos will apparently take time out from protesting the War in Iraq, gas prices, or Rutherford B. Hayes' controversial presidential election victory over Samuel J. Tilden in 1876, to travel to Oxford and take on the Rebels. José hopes for the best, but expects the worst. A win would bring a game versus either Nebraska (John J. Pershing) or Charlotte (Clay Aiken).

Finally, José would be remiss if he did not mention that although he wishes nothing but abject failure to The School Whose Name Shall Not be Spoken in all of their athletic endeavors, he is grateful that none of their fans got carried off by a twister.

My name is José Valdez IV and these are my thoughts.

Notes:

- **The reference to not wanting to talk about the fact that he used to be in the CIA is from *Vacation*.**

- **I really was in a group that participated in "The Cup" for a few years. We got together once a year to compete in various athletic contests. Eventually kids and our old age conspired against us and we discontinued the event. Bob Mims still has the trophy from the final one.**

- **I was very frustrated by the basketball season. I obviously had gotten my hopes up early in the season, against my better judgment, and the wheels just came off.**

- The "carried off by a twister" is a *Raising Arizona* reference. This was in regards to the tornado that hit the Georgia Dome while State was playing in the SEC Tournament.

José's Thoughts on the NIT Final Four

It certainly is exciting for the Rebels to be playing in the famed Madison Square Garden. Many may not be aware that the current Garden is actually the fourth incarnation of the arena and has been in use since 1968. It is the home of the New York Knicks basketball team and the New York Rangers hockey club. The Garden has been the site of numerous political conventions and featured concerts from legendary artists such as Elvis Presley, Led Zeppelin, The Who, Bruce Springsteen, The Rolling Stones, The Isley Brothers, Kiss, Bob Marley, Rush, and Debbie Gibson. However, there is almost universal agreement that the greatest moment in Madison Square Garden history happened on January 23, 1984 when Hulk Hogan captured the World Wrestling Federation Championship belt by defeating The Iron Sheik. Who above the age of thirty-five doesn't remember where they were when they got the news of the Hulkster's victory? José can assure you there was much rejoicing in Santa Poco when word arrived around mid-March.

It is difficult to describe what this basketball season has been like for José. He could use the rollercoaster analogy, but that would be too easy, and he has already employed that method to describe the emotions of Houston Nutt, the football game against The School Whose Name Shall Not be Spoken, and Space Mountain (which happens to be an actual rollercoaster). The best way José can describe what this season has been like is to say that it is similar to that relationship you had with the girl your junior year of high school. You thought she was kind of cute so you asked her out. Things progressed from there and after you had been dating her a little while all of your friends started commenting on how hot she was. Unfortunately, somewhere along the way things started to go terribly wrong. She didn't find *This is Spinal Tap* humorous at all, and you showed up for a date dressed in leather pants and a headband like the lead singer for Loverboy. *Note: We are strictly talking in hypotheticals here. There is no surviving evidence that proves José ever did anything of the sort.* Anyway, despite these and other setbacks you stuck it out and might still be together today had her family not had to enter the witness protection program and move away just before your senior year. Still, you parted on good terms and have fond memories of your time spent with her.

Sorry. What was José talking about?

Ah yes. The Ole Miss basketball team. Suffice it to say, it has been somewhat of a rollercoaster ride.

"Will José, Jorge, and Paco be in New York for the Final Four?" you ask.

Alas, they will not. They were politely asked never to return to the city after a certain incident at Shea Stadium in 1988 when they employed biting, eye-gouging, and the sleeper hold to procure a Keith Hernandez hit foul ball from a thirty-two year old mother of three. *Note: The ball is prominently displayed on José's mantel at the present time. With the rotation they agreed upon, Jorge will get it next year and Paco in 2010. Perhaps you have seen Jorge in the years it has been in his possession. He attaches it to a chain and wears it as a necklace.* Please do not concern yourself regarding their ban from New York as José, Jorge and Paco have become accustomed to such things as they are also not welcome in the state of South Carolina, all Midwest Arby's locations, Rapids on the Reservoir, and First Baptist Mendenhall.

Regarding the Rebels semi-final opponent, Ohio State, there are really only three cool things about the school:

- The Best Darn (José is trying to use less profanity) Band in the Land.
- Those Buckeye stickers on the football helmets.
- The cat from the movie Superfly attended there.

Other than those, they really don't have much going for them.

Concerning the game, José chooses not to make a prediction, as they have not gone so well lately. All he will say is that he is sure the Buckeyes are not excited about the prospects of potentially facing two SEC opponents. They have not fared so well against Southern boys lately.

My name is José Valdez IV and these are my thoughts.

Notes:

- One of my college roommates, who shall remain nameless, had a big crush on Debbie Gibson, thus the reference to her.

- I did NOT ever wear leather pants and a head band.

- The foul ball incident at Shea Stadium did not occur, however I did once race past a little kid at the old Texas Rangers stadium to secure a Bo Jackson batting practice home run ball. That probably doesn't sound so bad, but I already had two other ones and was twenty-two years old.

- I was married at First Baptist Mendenhall and as far as I know, am still welcome there.

José's Thoughts on the Ole Miss Baseball Season Thus Far

José apologizes for not sharing his thoughts recently. His Tivo had reached 99% full status so he needed to clear some space for the upcoming season of *Flight of the Conchords*. The last two weeks have been devoted to watching the *John Adams* miniseries, The VH1 *Behind the Music* episode featuring Metallica, season three of *The Jeffersons*, and *Throw Mama from the Train*. Oh, and José has watched Super Bowl XLII about twenty more times, but he's not deleting that one.

It would be difficult for José to count the number of times he has been asked to interject some Haikus into his thoughts. He has not previously done so because José was not certain what exactly constituted a Haiku. After some extensive research, although there is some disagreement, it appears to José that a Haiku should be three lines, include some reference to a season, have seventeen syllables, and not make a hell of a lot of sense.

José begins his collection with the following three Haikus:

The ball sails higher
Springtime beckons José
Go to hell LSU.

The Winter cold
An orphaned deer seeks solace
Sherrill was the devil

A Summer day
Caterpillars

Does anyone have Jessica Alba's e-mail address?

Ok. That last one went over seventeen syllables. But seriously, does anyone have Jessica Alba's e-mail address? José has some photos he would like to send her.

Concerning the Ole Miss Baseball season, José has been successful in not allowing his emotions to get too high or too low. When things were going poorly he was disappointed, but was not overly despondent. It would not shock José if this team was to somehow miss the SEC Tournament, but neither would it surprise him were they to advance to the College World Series. When you can throw Lynn and Pomeranz out there back-to-back anything is possible.

That being said, the last couple of weeks have been enjoyable. The team seems to have gained some confidence and different players are beginning to step up. The Governor's Cup should be interesting because it's always nice to have the opportunity to administer a beating to The School Whose Name Shall Not be Spoken, but the weekend series against South Carolina is the big one. Being that it is on the road, José, Jorge and Paco will not be in attendance as everyone is aware that they are banned from the entire state. This has not proven to be too much of a problem, as other than a few Rebel athletic events, and the fact that the world's largest collection of outdoor sculpture (at Brookgreen Gardens) is located there, there is not much reason to go to South Carolina.

While on the subject of the Gamecocks, José would be remiss if he did not mention the fight Jorge and Paco got into after an Ole Miss-South Carolina basketball game in the mid 90's over the Tupac – Biggie Smalls feud. Jorge sided with Tupac and the West Coast rap establishment, while Paco defended the Notorious B.I.G. and the East Coast group. *Note: José didn't feel comfortable taking either side in this one, being that he is not a rap fan, and preferring not to have a cap popped in his #@%.* After many punches, kicks and some bloodshed, Jorge and Paco agreed to disagree.

My name is José Valdez IV and these are my thoughts.

Notes:

- The *Metallica Behind the Music episode* **is very interesting.**
- **I finally got to work in the Tupac reference after having to remove it from an earlier thought because of the Sports Guy.**

José's Thoughts

Please give forgive José if his thoughts appear less than coherent or offensive in this particular offering. He has been drinking margaritas from the Billy Brewer/Ed Murphy cup that he got at this year's Grove Bowl for a couple of hours now. *Note: Unfortunately the dude in line in front of José at the game got the last Steve Sloan/Bob Weltlich cup.*

What is José to say about this past weekend's baseball series with the Razorbacks? He has rarely been more frustrated than he was this past Saturday (unless you count every date he went on from 1981-1987). José must admit that he does not understand some of the decisions that are made by Coach Bianco. For example, he has watched hundreds of baseball games over the years, but never has he seen a team attempt to employ a sacrifice bunt with two men on base, while down by three runs, late in the game. Maybe there is some special tie-breaker José has not heard about where games lost by one-run somehow work in your favor. Otherwise he cannot understand why anyone would employ such a strategy. But there are plenty of other things José does not understand as well so perhaps it is just him. Other things he does not understand include, but are not limited to:

- How much you should tip at Sonic.
- Anything James Joyce ever wrote.
- Why any movie role requiring dialogue or range of emotion would be offered to Keanu Reeves.

Regarding the decision to sacrifice bunt with two men on and down by three runs, in José's humble opinion, this is why you have bench coaches. So they can keep you in check. It should work like this:

Head Coach: "I think we should sacrifice bunt in this situation. What do you think?"
Bench Coach: "I think that's the dumbest thing I've ever heard in my life."

The same approach, of having someone to keep you from making grave errors, is also applicable in this business world.

Company President: "I believe we should focus all of our efforts on asbestos development. What do you think Johnson?"
Johnson: "I believe you must be an idiot."

There are also plenty of examples in history where having a non yes-man would have been beneficial. To wit:

Robert E. Lee: "Pickett. I want you to take your men and charge up that hill."
Pickett: "No thank you."

Finally, everyone should surround themselves with such people to assist them in their personal lives. For example:

Jorge: "I heard Todd Wade and his girlfriend might be breaking up. I'm thinking about asking her out. What do you think Paco?"
Paco: "I think you should go for it."
Note: Oftentimes it is necessary to seek a third opinion.

Despite his frustration, José has not changed his opinion from the one he shared a couple of weeks ago. He would not be surprised if this team either missed the SEC tournament or made it to the College World Series.

My name is José Valdez IV and these are my thoughts.

Notes:

- **The reference to the old cups was in response to the multiple complaints posted on the message boards about Ole Miss**

selling cups with Ed Orgeron's picture on them at the Grove
Bowl.

- This thought includes the only time I've been critical of a
coach, but I was extremely frustrated by the bunting strategy
Bianco employed in one of the games. I'm glad we have him,
but I don't always agree with his decisions.

- I truly am confused by the tipping etiquette at Sonic, and as
was clear from the responses I got to this, am not the only
one.

- James Joyce is absolutely unreadable.

José's Thoughts

Please forgive José for not sharing his thoughts very frequently recently. In his defense, much of his time has been spent in the confessional booth acknowledging his tendency to consume large quantities of tequila, chase women of ill repute, and shout profanities while watching Ole Miss athletic events.

"But José," you say. "Have you not previously acknowledged that you are not Catholic? Why are you spending time in a confessional booth?"

Those are both good questions and José is glad you asked. Indeed José is not of the Catholic persuasion. However it has been his experience that Presbyterian ministers really don't want to hear all that crap. That, and the fact that he sometimes feels the need to brag a little, is what leads him to the confessional booth. If the series against Auburn goes badly this weekend, you will most certainly find José there again come Monday morning. However, if the series goes well, the same may apply.

Being that José is not the most perceptive person in the world, he recognizes that he was probably the last person to grasp the obvious similarities between the current Ole Miss Baseball season and the Battle of Trafalgar. What remains to be determined is whether the season will ultimately conclude with the team having more in common with the battle's winning side, England, or its losers, the combined Franco-Spanish fleets. One can only wish that our boys will more closely identify with the Brits. Of course as everyone well knows, the English commander, Admiral Lord Nelson was killed in the battle, so let's hope the analogy breaks down there.

Actually, the more José thinks about it, the current Rebel season does not in any way resemble the Battle of Trafalgar and he is surprised that you would think otherwise. England was the great sea power of the day (although Boyd's World had them at #2 in the power ratings) while France was the dominant military land power. So as you can see, there are no real applicable similarities between the battle and Ole Miss Baseball. José would probably liken the season more to the movie *Top Gun*, where a Scientologist fighter-pilot falls from grace (getting that guy from *ER* killed in the process) but redeems himself eventually. Of course José doesn't know how the season is going to end. It could very well turn out to be more like *The Shining* or *There Will Be Blood*.

José must admit that with the struggles of the baseball team his thoughts have drifted and he has not been able to focus entirely on the season. Things he has wondered about include, but are not limited to:

- Where is Fuzzy Huddleston?
- Will El Chupacabra make an appearance in the new *X-Files* movie?
- Does Coach Nutt define stalking in the same way Coach Kennedy does?

My name is José Valdez IV and these are my thoughts.

Notes:

- **Boyd's World is a pretty good website that gives a lot of information about College Baseball. It is done by a guy from The School Whose Name Shall Not be Spoken.**
- **I never did find out where Fuzzy Huddleston was.**
- **As it turns out, El Chupacabra did not make an appearance in the *X-Files* movie. That may have been why it was so terrible.**

José's Thoughts

José has been very busy lately attempting to figure out which channel on his DirecTV broadcasts CSS. He has yet to find it, but will continue trying until he does. José is extremely persistent. If you do not believe this is true, you need only ask the folks at José's local radio station. He has called at noon for the past 647 days requesting they play "Mexican Radio" by Wall of Voodoo. *Note: They have yet to play it.*

José cannot figure out this Ole Miss Baseball team. He previously stated that it would not surprise him if the Rebels did not make the SEC tournament, but it also wouldn't surprise him if they made it to the College World Series. The former has happened and José is sticking with his thoughts on the latter. The pitching is capable (emphasis on capable) of taking this team a long ways. This team has also been criticized for not having heart, but facing a must win last Saturday, they delivered, and after some said they needed to win a couple in the SEC tournament, they beat the #1 seed and followed that with a win in the most dramatic fashion.

The pressure is on Bianco to make the right decisions going forward on whom to start, when to pull his pitchers, who to bring in, etc. Unfortunately it is not an exact science. One must look for signs and go with your instincts in many situations. José is probably not the right person to be giving such advice though, as his decision-making process in selecting Wife #1 proved.

There were two women in José's life in the mid 1980's. One was an emotional train wreck who we shall call "Rosie". One November weekend José drove four hours to pick her up so that he could take her to the Egg Bowl the next day. In the process he missed seeing the Doug Flutie Hail Mary pass. José should have immediately recognized there was no future, but alas, he did not.

The other woman we'll call "Salma". She was rock solid in every area of life. A few months after the Flutie incident with "Rosie", "Salma" went to Chicago with a group for a girl's weekend. That Saturday all of the girls went shopping. That is all except for "Salma". José still recalls the phone call he got from her.

"Salma" - "What are you doing José?"

José - "About to watch the Cubs game on tv."

"Salma" - "Oh really? That's nice. Look for me. I'm in the bleachers."

Yes, while "Salma's" friends went shopping, she decided to go to Wrigley Field by herself and see the Cubs.

So which of these two do you think José ultimately chose for Wife #1? That would be the one who made him miss the Flutie pass. José reveals this only to serve as a lesson to those unmarried young men out there. It's all about sports. If you are in a relationship and any of the following occurs, she is the one.

- Calls you from Wrigley Field (or any Major League park for that matter).
- Goes to an Ole Miss game with you in a revealing dress, but still yells at the referee
- Tells someone "Hockey is an ok sport, but you really need to see it in person to fully appreciate it.
- Can recite the infield fly rule.
- Critiques the authenticity of the football scenes in "Remember the Titans".
- Describes a left-handed person as a "southpaw".
- Calls you to tell you she's going to be late and requests that you Tivo the game so she doesn't miss tip-off.
- Comments "We really should throw to the tight-end more often."
- Doesn't think traveling is called as often as it should be.

Conversely, if you are in a relationship and any of the following occurs, she is NOT the one.

- Causes you to miss the Doug Flutie pass.

- When you say "Coco Crisp", she thinks cereal, not Red Sox outfielder.

- Tapes over your recording of the 1999 Ole Miss-Auburn football game.

- Utters the phrase "They're on the 52 yard-line".

- Questions you for watching last year's Super Bowl for the fourteenth time.

- Tries to console you after a bitter defeat to Alabama on a ridiculous reversal by the replay official by saying "It's just a game."

Postscript: "Salma" has been happily married to a surgeon for fifteen years now and, three wives later, José falls asleep most nights with whatever version of "Law and Order" happens to be on television, while covered in potato chip crumbs.

My name is José Valdez IV and these are my thoughts.

Notes:

- **It never fails that anytime an Ole Miss game is on CSS someone posts asking what channel it can be found on DirecTV. (It's not on DirecTV).**

- **I have previously mentioned that there was indeed a girl who caused me to miss the Doug Flutie pass.**

- **I actually married the girl who called me from Wrigley Field. She was, and still is, Wife #1.**

- **My wife does question my insistence on watching last year's Super Bowl over and over.**

- **I probably had more responses from women to this particular offering than any other one I've written. Many listed things they had done that proved they were worthy companions.**

José's Thoughts on the Letter

José recently received a letter that he felt compelled to share, along with his response.

Dear José Valdez IV (If that is your real name),

I read your recent thoughts on Mississippi State University, or as you refer to it "The School Whose Name Shall Not be Spoken". Where do you get off making such comments? You stated that Bulldog fans obsessed over Ole Miss like you obsess over Salma Hayek and Chimichangas, but that is a load of bull crap. I couldn't care less what happens at your lousy excuse for a school.

You also made the comment that most MSU fans either secretly wish that they went to Ole Miss or hope that their children do. I'll have you know that does not apply to my husband or myself, and we have matching Bulldog tattoos that prove our loyalty. Once you become a Bulldog, you are always a Bulldog and there is no turning back. If you want to see a representative of everything that is great about Mississippi State just look at Ron Polk and his history of dedication to our fine school. (Note: Letter written in May).

As for your making fun of our school's "Step Into the Maroon" slogan, we are very proud of it and feel it properly captures what it means to be a part of the Mississippi State family. Believe me, if you had ever "stepped into the maroon" yourself, you would understand. But that could never happen because you are not our kind.

Anyway, I just want you to know that you typify what everyone hates about Ole Miss. You think you're better than me, when in fact you are a small, insignificant piece of trash that deserves nothing but scorn. As I live and breathe I will hunt you down and HAVE MY VENGEANCE UPON YOU!!!!

Sincerely,

Lady Bulldog47

P.S. Loved your thoughts on Alabama. Those people are a bunch of rednecks.

And José's response.

Dear Lady Bulldog47 (If that is your real name. Knowing some fans of The School Whose Name Shall Not be Spoken, there is a high probability that is indeed your given name),

José received your letter and wanted to take the time to respond. He found your words to be very hurtful. You see, José can take almost anything in the world other than criticism. Oh, and he doesn't like pain either. Other than those two, he is a solid block of granite.

In regards to thinking he is better than you, José must address this. You may have many things in your favor when compared to José. You may be able to quote more of Chaucer, witnessed more Jerry Lawler wrestling matches, be able to name more state capitals, be closer to your high-school graduation weight, had more documented UFO sightings, have a greater Leo Sayer record collection, had fewer alcohol-related incidents at church picnics, and seen Morgan Fairchild naked. Yes, you may have all of those categories in your favor, but it all comes down to the fact that you are a fan of The School Whose Name Shall Not be Spoken and José is an Ole Miss fan. Because of that, José is better than you.

Sincerely,

José Valdez IV

P.S. Thank you for the kind words on José's Alabama thoughts. Those people ARE rednecks.

My name is José Valdez IV and these are my thoughts.

Notes:

- **I did not receive such a letter, but you must admit, it isn't outside the realm of possibility.**

- **The thoughts were written shortly after Ron Polk lost his mind.**

- I actually did have to memorize Chaucer in college and I still remember some of it. It's not really anything you can work into everyday conversation though.

- The seeing Morgan Fairchild naked reference comes from an old *Saturday Night Live* skit with John Lovitz.

José's Thoughts on the 1977 Notre Dame Game

The year of 1977 was a great one for José as it was the year Carmelita Benitez slipped him the tongue and was also when he started attending Ole Miss football games. This was particularly fortuitous as it happened to be the year that the Rebels defeated the Fighting Irish of Notre Dame in a game that Ole Miss fans still talk about to this day.

José still recalls the Valdez family loading up the family truckster to make the voyage from Santa Poco to Jackson, Mississippi for the game. For those too young to remember, the Rebels once played football games in Jackson. This was primarily because Vaught-Hemingway had yet to be expanded and seated only 483 people. It was also safe to go Mississippi Veterans Memorial Stadium without fear of having a cap popped in one's @%$.

Ole Miss fans typically carried around small Rebel flags in those days, and when they were driving to games often fixed them to the antenna of their cars. José recalls that the Valdez family drove the entire trip with their Rebel flag flying at half-mast (Elvis had died just a month prior).

After making the legally required stop for all Rebel fans at the Stuckey's in Vaiden (Don't ask why it was necessary to go through Vaiden on a drive from Mexico to Jackson, Mississippi. Just go with José on this one), the Valdez family parked the truckster at UMC, and made their way in the sweltering heat toward the stadium.

Ole Miss was a significant underdog heading into the contest and José did not have high expectations for how things would turn out. He had however, built up a significant hatred for Notre Dame after José III

119

informed him that the Catholics killed Martin Luther and were also responsible for the energy crisis of 1973.

Years of tequila consumption have affected José's memory, but if he recalls correctly, that Notre Dame team came into the game on a 273-game winning streak and had won every National Championship since 1963. The team was coached by Knute Rockne and featured players such as Joe Montana (who sat on the bench the entire game), Paul Hornung, George "The Gipper" Gipp, The Four Horseman, Ross Browner, Alan Page, Rocket Ismail, Tim Brown, Dave Casper, and Mike Golic.

As previously mentioned, it was very hot that September afternoon, so much so that José did not pull his tube socks up to his knees as he ordinarily did. He should have considered that the Mississippi heat and humidity would have an impact on The Fighting Irish, but it did not cross his mind at the time.

Although, the offense would come through in the end, what José remembers about the game was the defense. Linebacker Brian Moreland, was named Sports Illustrated Defensive Player of the Week for his twelve tackles, two fumble recoveries and an interception. Charlie Cage contributed seventeen tackles, and one of José's all-time favorite Rebels, George Plasketes, added fifteen tackles of his own.

Despite the heroic defensive effort, the Rebels found themselves trailing 13-10 with 4:53 remaining in the game. Ole Miss quarterback Bobby Garner had played a solid game to that point, but he was beaten up and dehydrated. Coach Ken Cooper elected to insert Tim Ellis for the final drive. Cooper called Ellis to his side and spoke words of encouragement to his quarterback. José had a perfect view of the sideline and is a pretty good lip-reader. Although he cannot swear to it, José is fairly certain Cooper looked Ellis in the eye and said, "Was it over when the Germans bombed Pearl Harbor"?

The Rebels started at their own 20 yard-line, and on the second play of the drive, Ellis hit Curtis Weathers for a first down. Next came one of the great plays in Ole Miss history. Before the game, not many fans could tell you who L.Q. Smith was. Anyone who was there will never forget him. Ellis threw over the middle to L.Q., who caught the ball at the Rebel forty and didn't go down until he was at the Notre Dame twenty-two. Afterwards Smith had a fantastic quote, which José cannot remember exactly (again, the tequila) but was something along the lines of "I caught the ball and took off running. Fabris had a great block, and there were a couple of others guys who threw good blocks, but I didn't stop to catch their names."

After that play, there was no doubt the Rebels were taking it in for the touchdown. James Storey carried the ball to the ten yard-line and on the next play reached back to catch a ball thrown behind him and took it in for the score. Notre Dame fumbled on their first play after that. The Rebels added a field goal, and the final score was 20-13. It remains one of the great moments in José's life as a Rebel fan.

Note: After the game José III informed José that he had lied to him in order to properly motivate him for the contest. The Catholics didn't kill Luther. He had actually been carried off by a twister. Also, the energy crisis was entirely the fault of the Methodists.

My name is José Valdez IV and these are my thoughts.

Notes:

- **With no Ole Miss sports occurring in the summer, I contemplated whether to write anything or not. I made the decision to write about some classic games and other random topics.**

- **We were actually living in Oxford at the time and of course stopped at Stuckey's on the way down. Numerous people commented that they always stopped there as well.**

- **Of the Notre Dame players I mentioned, only Joe Montana and Ross Browner were actually on the team. Montana didn't play.**

- **I'm sure I don't have the L.Q. Smith quote exactly correct, but that is very close to what he said.**

José's Thoughts on the Powe Situation

José is taking a break from the eleven-day vigil that he, Jorge and Paco have spent outside the SEC offices decrying the treatment of Jerrell Powe. He cannot yet report on the effectiveness of their protestations, but having to listen to Phil Collins' "In the Air Tonight" over 1,300 times is bound to have some impact on Mr. Slive. (Although José has repeatedly told Paco this his "air drumming" of the song reduces the credibility of their cause).

As with many Ole Miss fans, José has followed the Powe saga closely. There have been times where he felt confident that Jerrell was about to be cleared to play, and other times when he abandoned all hope. It now seems apparent that the ordeal will soon be wrapped up once and for all. Either he'll be cleared to play in 2008 or he will never see the field as an Ole Miss Rebel. *Note: This is just José's opinion. He has been wrong in the past. For example, his belief that he could attend the 1987 Chi-O Riverboat Spring Formal without a date and no one would notice proved to be egregiously incorrect.*

It occurred to José recently that if Powe is allowed to play and becomes a star, how similar his story will be to that of Roy Hobbs of *The Natural*. Other than the fact that Hobbs played baseball, was white, got shot by a deranged woman, became involved with another woman of questionable character, was offered a bribe to throw the pennant clinching game, rose from a hospital bed to play in said game, found out during the game that he had a son with his hometown sweetheart, and hit the winning home run off the lights setting off a fireworks display. But for those few things, it is exactly the same story. One can only hope that the ending is similar. *Note:*

José hopes that it ends like the movie version. The real ending in Malamud's novel is quite another thing altogether.

Another thing that recently occurred to José is how very long this situation has dragged on. Since signing day in February of 2005, when it first appeared that Powe would be suiting up for the Rebels, somewhere between 6.5-8.3% of José's life has transpired. (José is not quite sure how to calculate this. Suffice to say it's been a pretty damn long time).

To give a better perspective as to the duration of this saga, José lists below a sampling of the plethora of significant events that have occurred in his life and the world at-large since Powe signed his letter of intent in February of 2005.

- February 15, 2005: The website YouTube is launched.

- February 16, 2005: Jorge and Paco are permanently banned from posting videos on YouTube.

- June 23, 2006: Aaron Spelling dies. (José has heard it theorized that Spelling is the man most responsible for the cleavage we now see at Ole Miss. Showing cleavage was not a generally accepted practice on campus until his show *Beverly Hills 90210* reached its peak. Thus, his contribution to our society cannot be underestimated, and any Saturday in the Grove during football season bears witness to this. RIP Mr. Spelling).

- December 13, 2006: The Chinese River Dolphin officially becomes extinct. (Fortunately in April of 2008 the Bolivian River Dolphin was identified as a new species, so we're all square on the River Dolphins).

- January 14, 2007: Wife #3 files divorce papers with José citing "irreconcilable libidos" (She was a pirate hooker).

- June 1, 2007: A 2,000 year-old melon is discovered in Japan. (José is crappin' you negative on this).

- September 15, 2007: While passing through Canton, José stops at the Stone Pony for some adult beverages. As it happens, it is the night of a karaoke contest and he finishes fourth for his rendition of "Thunder Island".

- November 30, 2007: Evel Knievel dies. Jorge attempts to honor his memory by jumping his motorcycle over fifteen lawn chairs.

- December 10, 2007: Jorge is released from the hospital.

- March 22- April 12, 2008: After a five-game Rebel baseball losing streak happens to coincide with José's brief flirtation with parting his hair on the side, he goes back to the tried-and-true middle-part and the Rebs promptly real off nine straight victories.

As for Jerrell Powe, José has great admiration for the effort he has made to become eligible to play football at Ole Miss. Had José showed the same type of determination in his own life he may have achieved much more success and would probably be referred to as "eccentric" rather than just "idiot".

My name is José Valdez IV and these are my thoughts.

Notes:

- **Seriously, didn't every guy "air-drum" to "*In the Air Tonight*"?**
- **I did not attend the Chi O Riverboat formal in 1987. I did in 1989 though, and ended up marrying my date.**
- **I actually had not read Malamud's novel when I wrote this, but knew the ending was bad. I felt guilty about referencing it though and have read it since writing these thoughts.**
- **The "pirate hooker" reference is from *Anchorman*.**

José's Thoughts on the 1983 Egg Bowl

November 19, 1983. The Battle for the Golden Egg. The Immaculate Deflection. Good times for José. There were 59,783 fans at the game and José was one of them. In fact José III rented a large van to take to the game, so Jorge, Paco, their classmate Javier, and Paco's cousin Sheldon could all attend the game together.

José remembers that weekend very well because he played his final high school football game the night before. His Santa Poco Academy Fighting Luchadores came into the game with their arch-rivals, the Angry Friars of Saint Xavier, with an 8-1 record. Saint Xavier was unbeaten and the defending Mexican champions. The winner would advance to the playoffs as there were no wild-cards in Mexico in those days.

Anyway, without going into the dreadful details, José's Luchadores lost 21-13. Since Jorge, Paco, and Javier were on the team as well (Sheldon went to public school and repeatedly commented on the inferiority of the private school football product), the drive to Jackson for the Egg Bowl was not a pleasant one. José desperately needed a miracle to cheer him up. Little did he know that one was forthcoming.

For those too young to remember the game, you cannot appreciate how big it was at the time. The Rebels had gone eleven seasons without a bowl appearance and although they entered the game with a 5-5 record, it had been made clear that were they to defeat The School Whose Name Shall Not be Spoken (TSWNSNBS for the remainder of these thoughts) they would receive an invitation to the Independence Bowl.

Although they were a major rival, there was not the same level of animosity between Ole Miss and TSWNSNBS in those days that there is today. The TSWNSNBS readily accepted their place in the collegiate landscape, even embraced it (a position far below that of Ole Miss and more on par with a Georgia Southern). This was before the lying, cheating, snake in the grass Jackie Sherrill made an appearance on the scene. *Note: The accurate accounting of his evil deeds will likely never be known. In all probability he shot Tupac.*

The Rebels were a clear favorite heading into the game based on their four-game winning streak and the fact that TSWNSNBS came in with a 3-7 record. José was not concerned when Artie Cosby (remember that name. He will factor in later in the story) put TSWNSNBS up 3-0 late in the first quarter on a 19-yard field goal. He became somewhat worried when John Bond put the Rebels in a 10-0 hole with a quarterback sneak five minutes into the second quarter. After the lead increased to 17-0 José began to question whether Jesus loved him.

Timmy Moffet gave Rebel fans some hope when he returned a punt 66 yards for a touchdown with just over a minute to play in the first half. However, whatever momentum Ole Miss seemed to have, disappeared in the third quarter as TSWNSNBS stretched the lead to 23-7. That's when things started getting crazy.

Three plays after recovering a fumble, on the first play of the fourth quarter, Rebel fullback, Arthur Humphrey attempted to dive over the line on third and a yard. The ball was knocked loose and went flying backwards where quarterback Kelly Powell picked it up and ran around the right side into the end zone for the touchdown. It was now 23-14.

On the next possession TSWNSNBS fumbled again and three plays later Powell hit Moffett for a touchdown. With 11:26 remaining the score stood 23-21 and the place was rocking.

The next series Joe Hall (who had a huge fumble recovery at Tennessee earlier in the year to help turn the season around) intercepted a Bond pass and returned it to the 18-yard line. Three plays later Neil Teevan kicked a field-goal to put the Rebs up 24-23. It was now just a matter of holding on for the final ten minutes.

José was a young fan then and didn't know any better. He was convinced that the Rebels were going to win the game at that point. The twenty-five years since have made him a pessimist of the most extreme order. What he wouldn't give to go back to the naivety and optimism of his youth.

José learned an important life lesson that day. Never assume a game is over, because you know what it means when you assume. *Note: Actually José doesn't know what it means when you assume, but he has heard that said on many occasions. He assumes you know what it means.*

That particular life lesson goes along with a few others José had picked up a long the way, which include, but are not limited to:

- Do not, under any circumstances, come back from a good date in college and announce to your roommates "I feel like a butterfly." It will be repeated in group situations at your expense for the rest of your life. (Example: "Man this milkshake is good. I feel like a butterfly."

- Ferrets don't like cucumbers.

- Betting on games involving Ole Miss athletic teams (either on or against them) is a sure way to end up either in the poor house or an insane asylum.

- It is no longer cool to wear Sun Britches at the beach. (Learned last week).

- Sparky Reardon does not find streaking past the Tri Delt house to be amusing in any way, shape, or form.

José apologizes for the digression. Where were we? Ah yes, the Rebels were up 24-23 and things seemed to be looking good.

Ole Miss got the ball back and drove deep into TSWNSNBS territory, but Kelly Powell fumbled at the 20-yard line with 4:50 left in the game. Thus began an excruciating drive down the field with a winning season and bowl hopes resting in the balance.

With just over a minute left the ball was now on the Ole Miss 15-yard line, well within field goal range. After two John Bond sneaks picked up five yards there was about half a minute remaining. The Rebels called time out as Artie Cosby marched onto the field.

It would be difficult to describe the range of emotions that transpired for all Rebel fans in the following sequence. The team had come from a 1-5 record and a 23-7 deficit during the game and now faced the near certainty that it would end in a crushing defeat.

José's seat was almost even with the goal-line at the end of the stadium where the kick was attempted. He watched the ball rise high above the uprights. He does not remember feeling the wind, but will never forget the sight of the ball, a few yards short of the goal post, begin to spin in mid-air, not advancing forward or backward. Then it dropped towards the earth.

Pandemonium on the field and in the stands.

José yelled to Jorge, "José did not just see what he thinks he saw?!?"

Jorge replied, "Yes. José saw it!"

It remains one of the great moments in José's life. He has rarely questioned whether Jesus loved him after that day. (But when he did, it usually correlated with an Ole Miss athletic event). The drive back to Santa Poco was one of great rejoicing and for the first time in his life, José did not have to listen to José III talk about the glory years. *Note: The glory years commentaries resumed in 1984, and but for a brief respite in 2003, have remained steady since then.*

My name is José Valdez IV and these are my thoughts.

Notes:

- **My Dad did rent a van to take a bunch of my friends with us from Pensacola to the game.**

- **I did play my last high school football game the night before. We lost the district championship to our arch-rivals, Woodham High School, who was ranked #2 in the country, by a score of 21-13. We finished 8-2 and didn't make the playoffs. Still bothers me. To put it into perspective, my old high school, Tate, went 4-6 last year and still made the Florida playoffs. There is no justice.**

- **I really had a roommate in college come back from a date and make the "I feel like a butterfly" statement. I immediately ran down the hall and told everyone I found. He is a good guy so I will not reveal his identity.**

- **The "ferrets don't like cucumbers" quote is from Mike Myers.**

- **My seat was even with the goal line. That kick is still the most remarkable thing I've ever seen at a sporting event.**

José's Thoughts on the Summer

Before José shares his thoughts on the Summer, he feels the necessity to reiterate his hatred for all things LSU. This was reconfirmed for him on the recent Valdez contingent beach vacation. Due to the necessity to take the family dog Madrid (Named for Miguel de la Madrid), José did not stay at his normal vacation spot. *Note: José names all of his dogs after Mexican presidents. So it was reasonable to expect him to name one for the president responsible for entering Mexico in the General Agreement on Tariffs and Trades (GATT).*

The place where José did end up staying this year was overrun with supporters of Louisiana State University-Baton Rouge. It was difficult for him to tell if he was at the beach or the fair because the crowds are very similar. At least twenty people in his immediate vicinity had been featured on *COPS* at one time or another. Now José knows that there are some decent looking women who attended LSU or are Tiger fans, but apparently none of them, made the trip this year. You were more likely to see a 220 lb. woman in a thong with a tattoo of Mike the Tiger on her left buttock than you were to see a babe.

José writes this as a favor to you. If you are not a fan of either team, but are planning a beach trip in the near future, do the research and find out where the Ole Miss women will be staying. If this location proves to be beyond your current financial means, José suggests that you begin selling your plasma. (It's not that painful).

Back to the matter at hand, because the summer is such a slow time for Rebel sports, just as with many of you, José has passed the time writing poetry, working on a Papier-mâché replica of Stonehenge, and siphoning gas from vehicles with "Free Tibet" bumper stickers. *Note: Unlike many of you, part of José's Summer was also spent fulfilling his community service obligation to the dear people of Toccopola, Mississippi.*

Some people have approached José this summer and inquired whether he has plans to stalk Coach Nutt the way he does Coach Kennedy. José has given this a lot of thought, but from his experience, he has found that it is virtually impossible to stalk more than three people at a time. Considering José's current obligation to Coach Kennedy, Salma Hayek, and Billy Squier, he just doesn't have the time to adequately stalk Coach Nutt. He will have to settle for just dressing like him every day. *Note: Billy Squier has been a little too overly accepting of being stalked so there could be an opening soon.*

Summer is also a time for building expectations for the coming football season. It is hard not to get excited about what might happen in 2008, but if José has learned anything over the course of his life (other than the fact that only about 15% of Ole Miss girls will fall for the old "I'm the Pike Calendar photographer guy" trick) it is never to get his hopes too high when it comes to Ole Miss athletics.

My name is José Valdez IV and these are my thoughts.

Notes:

- **I do name my dogs after Presidents. My dog at the time of this offering was named Truman. I previously had a Lincoln.**

- **I was on vacation when I wrote this and my experience with LSU fans there was very similar to what I described.**

- **I've never actually attempted the "I'm the Pike Calendar photographer guy" trick, but I wish I'd thought of it years ago.**

José's Thoughts on Powe Gaining His Eligibility

Who will ever forget where they were on July 28, 2008 when they found out that Jerrell Powe had finally been cleared and would suit up for the Rebels in the upcoming season? José happened to be hiding in the locker-room at Fitness Lady in Ridgeland when he got the call from Paco delivering the wonderful news. Unfortunately his "We Built This City on Rock and Roll" ringtone gave him away and he was promptly escorted from the premises. Nevertheless, José exited with his head held high and in good spirits.

As he is sure was the case with most of you, the first thoughts that went through his mind (other than "Dammit. José wishes his cell phone was on silent) were from the William Butler Yeats poem "The Blessed":

> 'O blessedness comes in the night and the day
> And whither the wise heart knows;
> And one has seen in the redness of wine
> The Incorruptible Rose,

Of course José could be way off base here and you may have been actually thinking of Alfred Lord Tennyson's poem "The Captain" (although that would be rather silly of you as the Yeats poem is more applicable).

Although José certainly expects great things from Powe, he is going into the season fully recognizing that it may take some time for him to become the dominant player everyone is hoping for. José is taking this approach because he knows what it is like to be saddled with unrealistic expectations. For example, you cannot put José in a room full of beautiful women, serve him tequila, and expect him not to do or say something inappropriate within fifteen minutes.

Things have definitely been looking up for José recently. Between the Powe news and the discovery of the video of The School Whose Name Shall Not be Spoken's orientation, it has been a good few days. *Note: Since viewing the video, José has been diligently attempting to discover his very own "Dog Pound Rock" with no success. Rest assured that should he locate it, some sort of outpatient surgical procedure may be required.*

As for Mr. Powe, the moment he steps on the field for the first time, he will become one of José's all-time favorite Rebels, (along with Patrick Willis, Eli, Deuce, George Plasketes, Buford McGee, Jamie Holder, Chucky Mullins and a few others). That will not change whether Powe ends up a 3-time All-American or a role-player, because his desire to be a Rebel and the determination he has demonstrated to get to where he is today is unlike anything José has ever seen.

Here's to you Jerrell Powe!

My name is José Valdez IV and these are my thoughts.

Notes:

- **I got a funny response to this thought from someone saying that his granddaughter was a member of Fitness Lady and that he would now warn her to watch out for me.**

- **That "Dog Pound Rock" orientation video is quite humorous.**

- **Although Powe has yet to live up to the incredibly high expectations to this point, I still believe he'll be a major contributor in the coming years and I do have tremendous admiration for him.**

José's Preseason 2008 Football Thoughts

José apologizes for not sharing his thoughts in recent weeks. As you probably surmised, he was bewildered and disturbed to discover the recent *X-Files* movie featured no appearance by El Chupacabra. (Yes, José was one of the 347 people who actually saw the movie). How the producers of the film thought they could come out with a movie to compete with *The Dark Knight* and not even have a cameo appearance by EC is beyond comprehension. José encourages you to continue your boycott of the film.

Unfortunately, tequila alone was unable to assuage José's bitter disappointment. However, tequila AND the 1978 Sports Illustrated Swimsuit edition seem to work fairly well. (Cheryl Tiegs. Fishnet bathing suit. If you were in junior high then you know what José is talking about).

But José digresses. In less than two weeks a new era in Ole Miss football commences. If you were paying attention, the most recent era wasn't all that great. In fact it cost José his third marriage. *Note: In the interest of full disclosure, José acknowledges that alcohol, promiscuity, and their opposing views on predestination may have also been contributing factors.*

So what kind of season will the Rebels have in 2008? José isn't sure. But those who know him understand that he tries to keep his expectations low. He has not always been a pessimist, but fate and the prejudices of others have conspired against José to make him one. Several things that have contributed include, but are not limited to:

- The Ole Miss football seasons of 1976, 77, 78, 79, 80, 81, 82, 84, 85, 87, 88, 91, 93, 94, 96, 04, 05, 06, 07.

- His 1988 Phi Mu Spring Formal date. (This was when José first employed the old "fake pass-out" trick. It has proven to be useful on numerous occasions since).

- *The Mayor of Casterbridge*

- Seeing Jerry Lawler and Paul Orndorff dining together at Rendezvous during their supposed "feud".

- The Crusades

- Milli Vanilli

- Wives 1, 2, and 3

- Mistresses 2, 4, and 7.

Still, José wants to believe. He wants to believe that Jevan Sneed will be another in a long line of great Ole Miss quarterbacks such as Conerly, Gibbs, Griffin, Elmore and Manning. He wants to believe that one of this group of running backs will add their name to a list that includes Dottley, Flowers, Adams, McGee, and McAllister. Perhaps a linebacker will emerge who is worthy to be mentioned among the names of Grantham, Herrod, and Willis. José also hopes that this corps of defensive lineman develops into a group that will be spoken of in reverential terms for as long as football is played at the University of Mississippi. Finally, José can dream that in twenty years or so, many tears will be shed when Coach Houston Nutt retires and a statue of him is unveiled outside Vaught-Hemingway-Nutt stadium.

José also hopes that Lawler and Orndorff were just discussing how much they hated each other.

My name is José Valdez IV and these are my thoughts.

Notes:

- **The "fate and the prejudices of others" line is from *Raising Arizona*.**

- **I did once employ the "fake pass out" trick. I'm not proud of it, but desperate times call for desperate measures.**

- **I did not see Lawler and Orndoff together, but it could have happened.**

José's Thoughts on Memphis State

You are probably like José in that you have grown weary of summer and are ready for football to begin. Once your Netflix queue reaches the stage where you are being shipped season four of *Charles in Charge* you most likely need something else to occupy your time. Might José suggest reading the collected works of Graham Greene? (Or just read one of them seven times because they all seem to involve Catholicism, espionage, moral failures and a tragic ending. In fact, remove the Catholicism and you pretty much have the José story.)

Well deliverance from your boredom is on the way and it comes in the form of what seems like an entirely new Ole Miss football program. New coach. New quarterback. New running backs. New 37 year-old defensive lineman (Well it feels that way), New scoreboard. New mascot. Wait, scratch that last one. However, if it is ever determined that we have no alternative but to choose a new mascot José would like to go on record as preferring the Flying Elvises.

The opening opponent of the Nutt era is the University of Memphis Tigers. Memphis was originally named West Tennessee Normal School. It later became West Tennessee State Teachers College before becoming Memphis State College, then Memphis State University, and its current name, the University of Memphis. It obviously has a difficult time deciding on what it should be called. In other words it is the Puff Daddy, P-Diddy, Diddy, Sean "Puffy" Combs of colleges. However, all self-respecting Rebels will always refer to the school as Memphis State.

Memphis State is most known for producing two things; Wink Martindale and Keith Lee's jheri curl. The former has been the host of fifteen different television game-shows, including the classic *Tic Tac Dough*. The latter was a glossy, shimmering, tour de force of a hairdo, the likes of which may never be seen again. José is convinced that Memphis State later went on probation and had their 1985 Final Four appearance officially vacated because of the amount of money Keith Lee required to remain flush in Soul Glo.

There is a great story (perhaps apocryphal) about Lee's exchange with a certain reporter:

Reporter- "Keith, you are a physical education major, correct?"
Lee- "No man. P.E."

It is entirely possible that never really happened, but José likes that story and wouldn't bet money that it didn't.

José actually contemplated attending Memphis State at one point in his life, but after giving it much thought, decided to go on to middle school instead. It proved to be a wise decision as José probably would not have fit in as well there since he does not own the requisite number of blue jean shorts. (José owns five pairs. Their preference is that you have one for each day of the week).

Memphis State is expected to bring approximately 4,000 fans to the game, a collection of Philistines which fortunately only invades Oxford every other year. José is most definitely in favor of ending this one-sided rivalry. Ole Miss should not support such a lowly Conference USA program. It is a no-win situation for the Rebels as beating them brings no more glory than a victory over JA or Jackson Prep would. (Both of which are better coached than Memphis State). As you know, Memphis State is coached by the classy Tommy West, who yelled profanities at Rebel fans last year, surprisingly none of which included José, Jorge or Paco. *Note: Jackie Sherrill is the only coach to curse at them (at an infant baptism. Long story. Don't like to talk about it).*

As for the actual game, José will not make a prediction as he has no idea what to expect. He is cautiously optimistic, but then again he felt pretty good when the Rebels jumped up 21-0 on Alabama in the 1989 game, and many of you recall how that turned out. Still, hope springs eternal.

My name is José Valdez IV and these are my thoughts.

Notes:

- **I am a Graham Greene fan, but must admit that many of his books have very similar themes.**

- The Flying Elvises reference is from *Honeymoon in Vegas*.

- The Soul Glo reference is from *Coming to America*.

- I can't confirm that Keith Lee quote is accurate, but I believe it to be true.

- In the 1989 Alabama game the Rebels jumped out to a 21-0 first quarter lead and we were talking Sugar Bowl in the stands. The final score was 62-27 Alabama.

José's Thoughts on Wake Forest

Before sharing his thoughts this week, José feels it is necessary to dispel the rumor currently circulating that he was the person arrested after being found passed out naked in the circle this past Saturday. Now José isn't claiming he was not naked in the circle, just that he wasn't the person who passed out and was arrested. Give José a little credit.

José cannot recall the last time he had as much fun at an Ole Miss football game as he had last Saturday. In fact, José can count on one hand the number of experiences that were that enjoyable which did not in some way involve Carmelita Benitez and/or an REO Speedwagon concert. It was a great beginning to the Houston Nutt era, one that provides hope for even greater things to come.

On to Wake Forest. As has been previously discussed, José feels it is extremely important to summon the proper level of animosity for each Rebel opponent. This week proves to be one of those times that it is especially difficult to accomplish said objective. What is not to like about Wake Forest? They are a fine school, in a beautiful part of the country. They play the game the correct way and have one of the top coaches in the country. Even Brian Piccolo of *Brian's Song* fame went to school there. However, the primary reason it has proven so difficult to hate Wake Forest is because the school is in Winston-Salem, North Carolina and as everyone is aware, the very first Krispy Kreme donut shop was located there, so their contribution to our society, and civilization as a whole, can never be adequately calculated.

If José were forced to choose between tequila and Krispy Kreme donuts it would not be an easy decision. Jose has spent some time living north of the Mason-Dixon line, where Dunkin Donuts is the breakfast cake of choice, and they make some fine donuts (in José's opinion there is no such thing as a bad donut) but to put things in proper perspective, Dunkin Donuts is the Drew Barrymore of donuts; pleasant and satisfying, not something you would turn down if given the opportunity. Krispy Kreme is the Salma Hayek of donuts. Something you lie awake at night thinking about.

But José digresses. What reasons can be found to hate Wake Forest this week? Might José offer a few possible suggestions? You may not find them all good reasons to despise the Demon Deacons but Jose encourages you to pick the one that best prepares you for this Saturday's action.

- They destroyed the Rebels 27-3 in Oxford in 2006 in a game that was not as close as the final score indicated. The weather was miserable, as the start of the game was delayed a couple of hours and it was one of the most depressing Ole Miss games José has ever attended.

- The school boasts of an A Cappella group, *Innuendo*, which is described as "a mixed gender group intent on bringing hotness back to music."

- Howard Cosell was born in Winston-Salem. Now José actually liked Cosell as his Monday Night Football halftime highlights were eagerly anticipated every week. In fact, José III allowed a young José to stay up until the highlights had been shown so this does not serve as a good reason for him to hate Wake Forest, but it might work for you.

- Maya Angelou was on the faculty at Wake Forest. You know how José feels about poems that don't rhyme.

- For 100+ years the school was affiliated with the North Carolina Baptist State Convention. Baptists are anti-tequila. José is pro-tequila.

Hopefully Hurricane Hannah will not interfere with the ballgame this Saturday, but José would be more than happy to have the game relocated to Oxford, or Simpson Academy if a more neutral site is preferred.

My name is José Valdez IV and these are my thoughts.

Notes:

- **I don't know that the quality of these thoughts were any better or worse than any of my other ones, but this one was** significant because someone posted it on the Wake Forest message board and it was well received. For the remainder of the football season the thoughts were posted there by someone on a regular basis. The thing that pleases me the most is that it has given fans of another school a favorable impression of Ole Miss.

- Someone did pass out naked in The Circle after the Memphis game. It was not me.

- That 2006 game against Wake Forest may have been my low point as an Ole Miss fan.

- I spent a year living in Boston and ate Dunkin Donuts on a regular basis. They are good, but definitely not in Krispy Kreme's league. I love their coffee though.

Jose Valdez III's Thoughts on Nutt's First Game

After last Saturday's victory José III requested that his thoughts on the current state of the Ole Miss football program be shared. The following selection is his actual words. Please keep in mind that he is very different from José IV. For example he does not practice the fine art of tequila consumption, has no documented Bigfoot sightings, and would not be able to identify Salma Hayek in a lineup. Despite these shortcomings, he is a pretty good fellow. José IV imagines that his thoughts echo those of many of his generation.

Saturday, August 30, 2008, was a very good day for a fast aging Jose Valdez III. To see the Rebels play the way they did against Memphis put a spring in the old geezer's step and almost made him feel young again. Jose went so far as to start reminiscing about the four years he was an undergraduate at Ole Miss.

Jose has a tendency to first remember the bad -- the riot, and the Texas girl who got Jose started smoking cigarettes and then broke his heart. Jose was young so his heart only stayed broken for two weeks. Ah, but the good – there was a much prettier girl, and the Rebels won 3 of their 6 SEC football championships during the years Jose matriculated as an undergraduate. The Rebels lost a total of 3 football games during those years. You can look it up; it was during the time Coach Vaught called the Glory Years.

In recent years Jose has despaired of living to see his beloved Rebs ever win another SEC football championship. Jose knows about Eli's senior year and TYING for the SEC West, but the Rebels didn't even play in the title game. Jose went into deep dark depression during the O years.

In fact, Jose thinks of that time as the nightmare years, as in William L. Shirer's, *The Nightmare Years* that chronicles his time as a reporter in Europe just before WW II. Shirer also wrote *The Rise and Fall of the Third Reich*. Follow the thought and you see how depressed Jose was becoming. (Now you know where Jose Valdez IV gets his literary bent. But, alas, the boy reads too much fiction and not enough history!)

But then came August 30 and a new day for Rebel football under a real Nutt. Jose plans to live at least as long as Jerry Reed, one of his country heroes. The recently deceased Reed lived 71 years; that gives Jose at least 5 more years. Based on only one game, Jose fully expects to live to see the Rebs play for and win another SEC championship. Jerry Reed died of emphysema, but Jose quit smoking 5 years after the Texas girl, so he is counting on more than 5 years with the prettier girl and on seeing more than one additional SEC football championship for his beloved Rebs. Jose has been transformed into a big time optimist. Let the old man dream!

I'm Jose Valdez III and those are my thoughts.

Notes:
- **My Dad did write these thoughts.**
- **He really, really did not like Orgeron.**
- **He is more of an optimist than I am. I still need time.**

José's Thoughts on Stanford

In 1972 the late comedian George Carlin introduced his famous routine on the seven words you can't say on television. José was not on television this past Saturday, but he can confirm that he said at least five of those seven words within three seconds immediately after the Wake Forest field goal sailed through the uprights depriving the Rebels of what would have been a glorious victory.

José wishes he were an optimist. He truly does. It would be nice to go into each weekend confident that a victory was on the horizon, but that is not how José rolls these days. Thirty-plus years of falling short have beaten José down.

So why does he even bother anymore? Why not just throw in the towel and find another school to root for?

Well, there are a couple of reasons. One is that this is the team that José III saddled him with many years ago (and José has cursed his name because of this on many occasions). José is nothing if not loyal.

The other reason, the one that actually gives José hope that someday things might be different can be summarized in four simple words: The Boston Red Sox. Now it may disturb some people to find out that José is a Red Sox fan and he apologizes for that (actually he doesn't apologize, but hopes you can overlook that fact if it bothers you). If the Rebels have frustrated José over the years, the Red Sox did so on an almost equal basis for about the same amount of time. José became a fan in 1975 and suffered through excruciating losses for many years, but his faith was finally rewarded in 2004. Three years later and the Sox were champions again. If the Red Sox can do it, then maybe, just maybe, an Ole Miss team can win a championship. And José is not being greedy. He's not even talking about a national championship. A simple SEC championship would suffice.

Then maybe José V can live long enough to see the Rebels capture the big prize.

But enough of José's lamentations. On to Stanford.

Despite the criticism he sometimes receives, José believes everyone can agree that Pete Boone should be commended for getting a Pac-10 team to visit Oxford and take on the Rebels. To José's knowledge, this has never occurred before. He also finds it ironic that one week after playing Wake Forest, the Rebels will now play a school whose mascot is a tree.

Speaking of things everyone can agree on, José does not typically discuss politics, as he is a person who tries to bring people together rather than cause discord, but he must say that surely all will concur that should Sarah Palin become the Vice President, she would without question be the most attractive VP this country has had since Spiro Agnew.

But José digresses. Back to Stanford. Every true sports fan has seen the famous "the band is out on the field!" play from the 1982 game with their arch-rival Cal-Berkeley. The Cal-Stanford rivalry is considered to be one of the better rivalries in the country. The two schools trade insults on a regular basis and each tries to make arguments as to which is superior. José would have to go with Berkeley. If you have an element on the periodic table named after you (Californium: Cf, atomic number 98) then that should end the discussion.

Still, Stanford is a school with a great academic reputation. The school boasts of 18 Nobel Prize Laureates, 4 Pulitzer Prize winners and 21 recipients of the National Medal of Science. (Ole Miss has had three Miss Americas and one Charlie's Angel, so in your face Stanford!) It is however, best known for the fact that Sigourney Weaver graduated from there. *Note: José cannot confirm whether or not she was actually a man when she attended.*

José has no idea how many fans Stanford will bring, but they should be welcomed to the Grove. Please keep in mind that west coast schools like to protest things though and you should be prepared to receive grief if you have anything with Colonel Reb or a confederate flag on it. Also, some of their fans might not appreciate you driving a vehicle that requires gasoline, wearing khakis, or using utensils when you eat.

Wait. What is that you are saying to José?

The Rebels play SAMFORD?!?!?!?

Son of a …..

They are Baptists right? Perhaps Ole Miss will fare better against these Baptists than they did against the North Carolina contingent.

Rebels-103 Alabama Immersionists-0

My name is José Valdez IV and these are my thoughts.

Notes:

- I was fully prepared to get some comments from people stating that the Ole Miss was playing Samford, and of course, there were a couple.

- I finally revealed that I am a Red Sox fan in this post. I expected some negative reaction to that, but did not receive any, at least not publicly.

- Kate Jackson was the Charlie's Angel who went to Ole Miss. I don't believe she graduated though.

- I believe that the Sigourney Weaver is really a man story is an urban legend, but I wanted to throw it out there. Adam Sandler referenced this possibility in one of the songs he sang on *Saturday Night Live*.

José's Thoughts on Vanderbilt Chapter Dos

So the Rebels did not reach José's predicted 103-point margin of victory over Samford. Perhaps he should consider only commenting on areas in which he has a certain degree of expertise. Unfortunately that would leave José with weekly thoughts limited to tequila and his vast piñata collection, (José has a plethora of piñatas) so he will continue to ramble aimlessly about things he knows very little about.

There are a couple of questions that José is asked more often than one might imagine.

The first is "José, what do you think about UFO's?" His standard response to this question is "José likes them." That typically ends the discussion.

The other question José is asked more than one might surmise is "José, what do you think about Vanderbilt?" He typically responds, "José doesn't think about Vanderbilt." But that isn't really true. Indeed he thinks about the school each year when the Rebels play them in football, baseball, or basketball. So why does José lie? He cannot explain it. It just seems to come naturally to him. The list of things José has lied about over the years includes, but is not limited to:

- His whereabouts the night The Warehouse burned down. Now in no way is José offering any admission of guilt. Let's just say after consuming seven Foster's Lagers downstairs at Forrester's that night, his memory is somewhat fuzzy.

- When he said he was sorry to Jefe Rodriguez after punching him in the eye in fourth grade. This occurred after Jefe insisted

146

that Jim Plunkett was a better quarterback than Archie Manning. His teacher made him apologize. José wasn't sorry then, and he isn't sorry now.

- His affection for Faulkner's *The Sound and the Fury*. José would like to be considered somewhat intelligent among the dinner party crowd, but honestly he doesn't understand a damn word of it.

- When he said he was sorry to Jefe Rodriguez after punching him in the eye last week at Buffalo Wild Wings. This occurred after Jefe said that Jay Cutler was a better quarterback than Eli Manning. His pastor made him apologize. José isn't sorry this time either.

José must also admit that any time he sees Ned Beatty he thinks about Vanderbilt.

"Why would you think about Vanderbilt when you see Ned Beatty?" you ask.

Well if you will stop interrupting José he will tell you. Did you happen to see *Deliverance*? (The feel-good movie of 1972).

It just so happens that the person who wrote both the novel and screenplay of the movie, James Dickey, is a Vanderbilt grad. So anytime José sees Ned Beatty, he unfortunately cannot suppress the "squeal like a pig" scene images from entering his mind and immediately wonders what the hell they must have been teaching at Vanderbilt for Dickey to write such a disturbing piece. Because of that scene alone José will never go whitewater rafting. In fact, he is convinced that the whitewater rafting business has lost approximately 2,000,000 potential customers over the years because of *Deliverance*. Turkish prison or whitewater rafting? Both sound equally unpleasant to José.

The game this Saturday is a huge one for the Rebels. Bowl hopes for both teams will be tremendously impacted by the outcome. A December visit to Shreveport (or anywhere for a bowl game) never sounded so good to José.

My name is José Valdez IV and there are my thoughts.

Notes:

- **"Plethora of piñatas" is from *Three Amigos*.**

- The UFO story comes from my father. When he was a young man his older sister asked him, "What do you think about UFO's?" He responded, "What do you mean what do I think about UFO's?" She replied, "Do you like them?"

- I did not burn down The Warehouse.

- I have been whitewater rafting. In fact I've been down the Chattooga, where they filmed *Deliverance*. I heard no banjo music on my trip, but was prepared nevertheless.

- The Turkish Prison reference is from the movie *Midnight Express*, which is every bit as disturbing as *Deliverance*.

José's Thoughts on Florida Chapter Dos

José is an idiot.

"Tell me something I didn't already know," you say.

Touché.

Perhaps he should rephrase. Once again José proved himself to be an idiot this past weekend. He broke his cardinal rule for being an Ole Miss fan. He went into the game this past Saturday expecting to win. Never, ever, under any circumstances, should José expect victory in an Ole Miss athletic competition. It is alright for José to go in hoping for a win. Even feeling that the Rebels chances are quite good is acceptable. Expecting victory is another story. Once again, José is not suggesting that you adhere to this same philosophy (unless maintaining your sanity is a personal goal), he has just found that this approach works best for him. This may change someday, but in the meantime he will stick with the plan. When the Rebels deliver a few big wins, then he will reevaluate his approach.

It is good that José did not share his thoughts within twenty-four hours of the conclusion of the game because they were not suitable for viewing by people younger than eighteen or those with any modicum of decorum. Unfortunately, the same held true for his thoughts seventy-two hours after the game as well. José now feels he can share his thoughts, but know that they have been edited for content. For the remainder of his thoughts you could probably substitute the profanity of your choice for any occurrence of the words "he", "and", or "the" and it would give a better picture of what José is actually thinking. For those who believed that José has been in isolation the past few days attempting to find solace in a bottle of tequila, you couldn't be more wrong. It was George Dickel. White Label.

The sad thing is that José had such high hopes heading into the season. The summer had gone especially well. For the first one in over a decade José was not either: charged with a crime, shot at by an ex-wife or girlfriend, or involved in an altercation with the Shriners. It is easy to see why José would feel things were starting to turn in his direction. Now to be clear, he is not prepared to give up on the 2008 season. There still remain opportunities to make it a memorable one. And he is certainly not ready to give up on Jevan Snead. He would be surprised if Snead ever has another game like he had against Vanderbilt.

As for Florida, it is especially challenging for José to proceed with any degree of confidence simply because of the many advantages the state of Florida has over Mississippi. To wit:

- Florida has animal theme parks such as Busch Gardens, Animal Kingdom, and Sea World. Mississippi has that zoo off of Highway 49 around Collins that features a mountain lion, a wolf, a three-legged dog and a proprietor of average height who bills himself as a "huge midget".

- Florida features numerous resorts where nudity is permitted. Mississippi has numerous locations in Tallahatchee County where people like to get naked even though it is not officially sanctioned.

- Florida has multiple thousands of high school football players, 75% of which run sub 4.5 40-yard dashes (or so it seems). Mississippi is the most obese state.

So why should José believe the Rebels have any chance whatsoever against a team from this state?

South Panola 28 Apopka 18.

Just hoping. Not expecting.

My name is José Valdez IV and these are my thoughts.

Notes:

- **I've since gotten to the point where I can go to an Ole Miss game expecting victory, but it definitely feels weird. In most cases I am cautiously optimistic.**

- I've never actually visited that Collins Zoo, but have driven by it 1,000 times.

- My favorite response to this selection was a post that read "Where are the locations in Tallahatchee County?"

José's Thoughts on South Carolina Chapter Dos

Jesus loves José!

Well if he doesn't actually love José, at least he doesn't appear to hold the same level of contempt for him that Mother Teresa did. *Note: Their feud began in Tijuana in 1989. She started it.*

Alas, José was not in Gainesville last Saturday when the Rebels pulled out their amazing victory over the Gators. (He was there for the game that Eli won), but his celebration was no less enthusiastic than it would have been had he been in the stands. In fact he would like to offer a sincere apology to Mrs. Janine Warner of Ridgeland, who was the first person he saw on the street after the game concluded. He does not normally try to slip the tongue to complete strangers. However should the Rebels win another game against a top ten team this year, he cannot promise it won't happen again.

Late in the day José, Jorge and Paco decided they should make the trip to Oxford to welcome the team back. Unfortunately they made a longer than anticipated pit stop at Proud Larry's and missed the team. So they settled for going to Coach Nutt's house around 2:00 AM. While standing out in his yard they did what any of you would have done had you been in the same position. They sang "Wonderwall" at the top of their lungs.

And all the roads we have to walk are winding
And all the lights that lead us there are blinding
There are many things that I would
Like to say to you
But I don't know how

Because maybe
You're gonna be the one who saves me
And after all
You're my wonderwall

To Coach Nutt's inestimable credit he came out and gave a warning that he had called the police, giving the group time to disperse. Coach Kennedy usually comes straight out discharging his weapon.

On to South Carolina.

When you hear "South Carolina" of what do you think? For José it is Preston Brooks. As everyone well knows, Brooks was the congressman from South Carolina who beat Massachusetts congressman Charles Sumner with a cane on the floor of the senate in 1856. Many are under the impression that it was politically motivated, but it probably had more to do with personal insults. Keep that in mind as you see Gamecock fans this weekend. They are a testy bunch. José recommends that you either remain cordial or carry a very big stick.

The only advantage José can come up with that South Carolina has over Mississippi is that there have been forty-two credible Bigfoot sightings in South Carolina according to the Geographic Database of Bigfoot/Sasquatch Sightings & Reports. (By comparison, Mississippi has recorded only eighteen such sightings, seven of which are from José. Six of those may or may not have been tequila induced, but the other one is completely legit).

José fully believes that the Rebel team has more talent than South Carolina, but the Nutt-Spurrier matchup will be fun to watch. As big as the victory was this past weekend, it must be followed up with a home win if this team is to accomplish what many thought they were capable of heading into the season. Hopefully the Florida game has converted the team into a group that now believes it will find a way to win when the game is on the line.

My name is José Valdez IV and these are my thoughts.

Notes:

- **There is no Janine Warner of Ridgeland. At least I hope not.**

- **I figured someone would suggest that I must have been a Pike, considering the Charles Sumner reference, but that did not happen.**

The Thoughts of José Valdez IV

- **I found it humorous that right around the time I wrote this the alleged "body of Bigfoot" was discovered. I knew it wasn't the real Bigfoot.**

José's Thoughts on Alabama Chapter Tres

Numerous people have contacted José to inquire as to his whereabouts and activities during the bye week. *Note: By "numerous" José means three. One of which he owes money to and the other two have been persistent in their efforts to obtain his membership in the new religious cult they are forming. It's a ground-floor opportunity and José would be third in command, so it is somewhat enticing. Chicks dig cult leaders.*

Actually, because he celebrated a birthday during the bye week, it was a time of reflection for José; an opportunity for him to look back on the successes and failures of his life thus far. Of course if one discovers during his time of reflection that he is in his forties and counts an intramural ultimate frisbee championship and top five finish in the 2004 Yalobusha County Texas Hold 'Em Tournament among his greatest accomplishments, depression and tequila consumption are sure to follow. And follow with a vengeance they did.

Despite the eye-opening self appraisal, José believes that better days lay waiting just over the horizon. Perhaps they will begin this weekend with a victory by the Rebels over the Alabama Crimson Tide. Those who know José well, understand that he holds the Tide in particular contempt. That has not always been the case, but after last year's game they have moved way up the list of teams that José despises. Now José does not hate every SEC team, but for those that he does, he can identify the exact point in time when his hatred took root.

Tennessee- When Peyton announced he was attending there.
Auburn- Upon Tuberville's cowardly exit.

155

LSU- When José first heard about Billy Cannon.
Arkansas- When they were admitted into the SEC.
Kentucky- Upon seeing Kyle Macy on the basketball court in shorts the size that Hooters girls now wear.
Vanderbilt- When they informed José that applying to go to school there would be a waste of both his time and theirs.
South Carolina- Saturday before last.
The School Whose Name Shall Not be Spoken- When brain activity commenced.

The Alabama Crimson Tide is coached by that paragon of virtue, Nick Saban. As for people that José hates, Saban sits comfortably in the top five. He currently occupies the three spot between Pol Pot and a certain bouncer from the Flora-Bama Lounge. Since Pol Pot is dead and can do no further damage, Saban is perfectly capable of moving ahead of him on the list. Should he pass Pol Pot, then Saban would have that Vince guy from the *ShamWow!* commercials squarely within his sights.

As for the game this weekend, might José suggest that if you are the praying kind, you offer up your requests that it not come down to an official's call? José would do so himself but he has found from experience that his supplications are generally not looked upon favorably for at least two weeks after he gets liquored up and e-mails pictures of himself in various stages of undress to the mothers of Jose V's 6th grade classmates. *Note: Seventeen fathers have threatened to beat the crap out of José, but on a positive note one mother sent pictures back to him. They have a date next Friday*

With the home loss to South Carolina, the Rebels need to win another road game or two and protect their home turf in order to have the type of season all thought possible after the Florida game. This week seems to be as good as any to get one of the road victories. Just don't put the Rebs on the cover of Sports Illustrated if they do pull it off.

My Name is José Valdez IV and these are my thoughts.

Notes:

- **I was on an ultimate Frisbee championship team. I've never been in a poker tournament.**

- **I didn't realize how much everyone else hated the *Shamwow!* guy until I wrote this piece.**

- Not wanting to be on the cover of *Sports Illustrated* is in reference to the jinx being at work. Of course after the Rebels defeated Florida and made the cover, they lost the next week to South Carolina.

- My son Wes was in 6th grade when I wrote this. I have not offended any of the mothers of his classmates, to my knowledge.

José's Thoughts on Arkansas Chapter Dos

"Of all sad words of tongue and pen the saddest are these, what might have been."

That John Greenleaf Whittier quote probably went through your mind shortly after the Rebel's narrow defeat this past Saturday. It did not go through José's mind, partly because, unlike you, he does not memorize quotes by Whittier, and also because at that point in time he was thinking about what dish goes well with Jägermeister. (He still does not know but can tell you that hot wings do not).

Many are calling the current Ole Miss squad "The best four-loss team in the country." José takes no solace in that and it is reminiscent of when The Wife Whose Name Shall Not be Spoken once referred to him as "not the biggest loser I've ever been married to." José would much prefer that the Rebs were "The worst undefeated team in the nation," or even "the ugliest one-loss team in the country." Hell, he would be happy with "an overrated 4-3 team" at this point. But, it is what it is.

Note: "It is what it is" has become the most overused saying out there, but similar to "This too shall pass", José has found that it is appropriate in almost any situation. For example, just this past weekend:

Jorge: "Sheesh José, look at your rug. You should have never let your dog eat those leftover chimichangas.

José: "It is what it is."

But José digresses. On to Arkansas.

It has been brought to José's attention that there is a José Valdez playing football for the Razorbacks. Unless Wife #1 has been keeping a secret for 20+ years (and that is not outside the realm of possibility), he is no relation to IV. Judging from his size though, José would guess that Andre the Giant is more likely to be the father.

José has spent much of his time the past few days contemplating the differences between Coach Nutt and Coach Petrino. They are many. He offers his observations on a select few of them which clearly demonstrate why the Rebels should be thankful to have Coach Nutt and the Razorbacks should be chagrined that they are saddled with Coach Petrino.

- Coach Nutt takes an active interest in the personal lives of his players.
- Coach Petrino takes approximately thirty minutes each morning trying to remember where he is and what team he is currently coaching.

- Coach Nutt has a personal library that includes the works of Faulkner, Shakespeare, Tolstoy, Hemingway, Dickens, McCarthy, McMurtry, Ambrose, McCullough and Willie Morris.
- Coach Petrino once read Sue Grafton's "P" is for Peril.

- Coach Nutt wept openly during the movie *Brian's Song*.
- Coach Petrino wept openly during the movie *Steel Magnolias*.

- Coach Nutt is fluent in seven languages: English, Spanish, Portuguese, Italian, French, Mandarin Chinese, and Arabic.
- Coach Petrino has yet to master the English language, consistently dangling his participles and finishing sentences with prepositions.

- Coach Nutt is involved in numerous charitable endeavors.
- Coach Petrino hates orphans. He hates all the orphans in the whole world.

- Coach Nutt's iPod features an eclectic mix of selections from Lynyrd Skynyrd, Grand Funk Railroad, Merle Haggard, Johnny Cash, U2, The Replacements, B.B. King, James Brown, and Bruce Springsteen.

- Coach Petrino's iPod features selections from Glass Tiger, Color Me Badd, Cher, Right Said Fred, Wham, Rockwell and Rick Springfield.

- Coach Nutt recycles.
- Coach Petrino uses Styrofoam products.

- Coach Nutt will knock back a shot of tequila after a big victory.
- Coach Petrino prefers mojitos.

- Coach Nutt is a humble man who attempts to direct any praise toward his assistant coaches and the players.
- Coach Petrino has a personalized license plate that reads "Saucy".

Note: José must admit that he made up part of the above. There is no conclusive evidence that Coach Nutt speaks Arabic.

The game against Arkansas this week is a big one for many reasons. Most importantly, the bowl hopes of this Rebel team hang in the balance and a win would put them in a much better position. The game is also meaningful because of the Coach Nutt factor. There is no doubt it will be an emotional day for the Ole Miss coach and he would like to demonstrate to Razorback fans that he is a better coach than the one they currently have.

It's time.

My name is José Valdez IV and these are my thoughts.

Notes:
- **My dog Truman's similar incident just days prior, inspired the chimichangas bit.**
- **I cannot believe Arkansas has a football player named José Valdez. What are the odds?**
- **The "hates orphans" reference is from *Nacho Libre*.**

- **I do have selections from the artists I attributed to Nutt on my iPod. I do not have any from those I attributed to Coach Petrino. But I bet he does.**

José's Thoughts on Auburn Chapter Tres

José was not at the Arkansas game last Saturday. José was at the infamous Valpo basketball game. Losing this one would have been worse. But alas, the Rebels somehow found a way to win and for that José is grateful. One could dwell on the plays that almost cost Ole Miss the game, or choose to focus on the big plays made that forced Arkansas to need a miracle in order to have an opportunity to pull out the game. After much consideration, José chooses the latter.

At some later point in time José will address the apparently new definition of the word "indisputable", because he has numerous thoughts on that subject. For now though, he moves on to Auburn.

All is not well on The Plains. The Coach Whose Name Shall Not be Spoken is catching a great deal of heat (which causes José no consternation whatsoever) for the lackluster performance by the Tigers thus far. The Tony Franklin System did not work. Perhaps they should have considered the Alan Parsons Project. The results could not have been that dissimilar.

Everything seems to be in place for a big Rebel victory, but you well know how that situation has played out recently. It is time that the Rebel football team won a big home game. Their success rate at protecting their home turf has approximated that of the Roman Empire's protection of their primary city over the course of its history. In fact, one could easily list a distressing Ole Miss loss at Vaught-Hemingway in the past few years that corresponds with every sack of Rome. To wit:

1999- Vanderbilt 37 Ole Miss 34 in OT. This was David Cutcliffe's first home game as the Ole Miss head coach. Cutcliffe came in with Rebels fans at a low point after The Coach Whose Name Shall Not be Spoken departed, and led the team to an Independence Bowl victory over Texas Tech. His first regular season game in '99 was an uninspiring 3-0 victory at Memphis. The honeymoon was over though after losing at home to Vanderbilt.

This is reminiscent of the Gauls defeat of Rome in 387 B.C. Of course the Gauls chose not to bury the dead after the battle and an epidemic broke out in the city, thus ending their siege. Similarly, Vanderbilt went on to have another crappy season after defeating the Rebels.

1999- Georgia 20 Ole Miss 17. The Rebels make a late drive deep into Bulldog territory and can win with a touchdown, but are at least in chip-shot field-goal range that would tie the game. Romaro Miller has a pass tipped that is intercepted just before hitting the turf and Georgia runs out the clock for the victory.

One can't help but think of Alaric and the Visigoths conquering of Rome in 410 A.D. when contemplating the '99 defeat at the hands of Georgia. The Romans had held off the siege on a couple of occasions prior through negotiations, but ultimately the city was sacked. Tens of thousands of Roman citizens fled after the defeat with many of them ending up in Africa. Similarly, José fled Vaught-Hemingway immediately after the Georgia loss, but only went as far as Grenada.

2001- Arkansas 58 Ole Miss 56 in seven overtimes. This was a particularly devastating defeat. It was Eli's first year as a starter. The Rebels came into the game with a 6-1 record and 3-1 in the SEC. They were significant favorites over the Razorbacks, had numerous opportunities to win, but ultimately couldn't close the deal. This game cost Ole Miss dearly as they finished 7-4 and out of the bowls.

Now you are probably thinking that the Arkansas game is just like the defeat of Rome at the hands of Geiseric and the Vandals in 455 A.D., but José would beg to differ. That really wasn't a significant upset. José would go with the 546 A.D. defeat dealt by Totila and the Ostrogoths. Nobody saw that one coming.

2003- LSU 17 Ole Miss 14. This was the most devastating of all. The Rebels were 6-0 in the conference. A win would give them the SEC West title and a berth in the championship game. The atmosphere was unlike any José has seen in his lifetime as an Ole Miss fan and the Rebs had their chances, but ultimately couldn't get it done.

José believes everyone can agree that the LSU game was almost exactly like the sack of Rome in 846 A.D. by the Saracens (or Arabs if you prefer), where even the Basilica of St. Peter was not spared from desecration. Damn those Saracens!

There have been numerous other excruciating home losses in recent years (Texas Tech 2003, Alabama 2007, Vandy 2008, South Carolina 2008 to name just a few), but unfortunately only a limited number of conquests of Rome during the years of the Roman Empire to correspond.

This is the biggest home game since LSU in 2003. As for the crowd, José has no problem with the comments made by some of the players this week. He has been guilty of not being as loud as he should on occasion, more because of nerves than anything else (nervous about the game and also about the possibility that someone in the crowd will identify him as the person who roamed the halls of the Chi O house from 1984-1988, pretending to be a house boy), but vows to turn it up this Saturday. If you typically sit on your hands, get up and be loud this Saturday. If you are normally loud, be louder. If an elderly woman sitting in front of you turns around and punches you in the eye because you are so loud, then by God, you've done your part.

Finally, not to boast, because José is nothing if not humble, but he would be remiss if he did not mention the personal e-mail José received from Coach Nutt requesting that he wear blue to the ballgame this Saturday. With that in mind, José kindly asks the rest of you to please wear another color as Coach Nutt apparently wants to be able to pick out José when he looks up into the stands.

My name is José Valdez IV and these are my thoughts.

Notes:

- **I make reference to "indisputable" because of the onside kick that was overruled in the Arkansas game. There is no way that there was indisputable evidence that the Razorback player had control of the football, but we've become accustomed to getting the short end of these reviews at Ole Miss.**

- **Bringing up The Alan Parsons Project was inspired by a scene in one of the *Austin Powers* movies.**

- All of the games I mention were incredibly painful losses. The Auburn win was hopefully a portent of things to come.

- The reference to an elderly woman punching you in the eye because of your loudness was inspired by a poster who apparently had this happen to him at the Arkansas game the week before. I thought it was hilarious.

- Coach Nutt composed an e-mail that was sent to fans that week requesting that they were blue. A poster on one of the message boards made it clear that I wasn't the only one to receive the e-mail.

José's Thoughts on Louisiana-Monroe

José offers his apology for not sharing his thoughts since the Auburn game. He actually just left the stadium moments ago.

Left. Forcibly removed. It is all a matter of perspective.

"But José," you say. "Do you mean to tell me that you have been in Vaught-Hemingway these past ten days?"

That is what José was trying to say before you interrupted him.

To say that he was excited after the victory over the Plainsmen from Auburn would be an understatement. In fact, José was so excited that he could not bring himself to leave the stadium. So the past ten days he has been hiding out during the day and going onto the field at night to reenact the entire game.

"You should have been able to do that in one night José," you say.

You are perceptive and ordinarily that would be true, but when José reenacts the game he must do so from every Ole Miss player's perspective. Each night he chooses one offensive and one defensive position and goes through every play from their point of view. This was easy to do because Jorge had Tivo'd the game and he fed José a description of each play through the headset (Cellular South of course) that he had "borrowed" from the coaches' box.

It is entirely possible that Jorge was doing tequila shots this past Thursday night when José was reenacting Jevan Snead's game because he has no recollection of Snead turning somersaults down the field after his first touchdown pass and giving The Coach Whose Name Shall Not be Spoken the finger, but since José did not have the video evidence in front of him to refute Jorge's assertion, he was forced to rely on his good word.

Anyway, José was all set to complete the final two positions this evening; offensive left guard and strong safety, but was discovered eating some leftover barbecue nachos in the concession stand by Langston Rogers, who immediately called security. *Note: Rogers has had it in for José ever since that whole daytime fireworks fiasco at Vaught-Hemingway last season.*

On to Louisiana-Monroe.

The University of Louisiana-Monroe Warhawks were known as the Northeast Louisiana Indians just a few years ago. Should hawks gain a primary spot on the endangered species list anytime soon, don't be surprised if they show up in Oxford demanding to be called the Ouachita River Area Non-Violent Placaters.

ULM is perhaps best known for being the alma mater of everyone's favorite college football studio host, Tim Brando. José actually saw Brando sitting in the stands at an Ole Miss-LSU baseball game in 1989. He was wearing gym shorts and tube sox that were pulled up to his knees. Even José gave up that look in the late 70's. José contemplated asking him if he was headed to the skating rink or an Olivia Newton John video shoot after the game, but he didn't want to give Brando additional incentive to poor mouth the Rebs.

The Warhawks come into Saturday's game with a 3-6 record. However, they lost by just one point at Arkansas, and everyone should recall that they won at Alabama last year. A victory by the Rebels almost certainly clinches a bowl berth. José cannot believe he just wrote that. It has been a long time since he could even contemplate such. To put in perspective how long it has been since Ole Miss went to a bowl game he offers you a list of some of the significant events that have occurred since the January 2004 Cotton Bowl.

- April 29, 2004: The last Oldsmobile rolls off the assembly line.

- October 27, 2004: The Boston Red Sox win their first World Series since 1918.

- October 10, 2005: Jorge, Paco and José go out on the town for what is planned to be a quiet, reflective celebration of José's 40th birthday.

- October 24, 2005: Jorge, Paco and José finally make bail.

- January 9, 2006: The Dow Jones closes above 11,000 for the first time since 2001.

- March 17, 2006: Salma Hayek gets naked in the movie "Ask the Dusk".

- September 5, 2006: Felipe Calderon becomes the new President of Mexico.

- September 6, 2006: José is removed as President of his homeowner's association in a coup d'état led by the Methodists in the neighborhood.

- April 11, 2007: Kurt Vonnegut dies.

- June 27, 2008: Bill Gates steps down as Chairman of the Microsoft Corporation.

- October 31, 2008: After a twenty-eight year quest, José finally locates a Salami action figure, thus completing his set of *The White Shadow* collectibles.

José is not taking a win over the Warhawks for granted, and implores you not to do so either. The Rebels need to finish strong as José would like to make a bowl trip this year. It is somewhat embarrassing for him to continue to wear his 2004 Cotton Bowl cap. Not as embarrassing as fans of The School Whose Name Shall Not be Spoken wearing their 2005 Egg Bowl Champion t-shirts (when they went 3-8), but embarrassing nonetheless.

My name is José Valdez IV and these are my thoughts.

Notes:

- **The daytime fireworks mention is in reference to the ones that knocked out the scoreboard at one of the home games the prior season.**

- **I spent my first year of married life in Monroe, Louisiana, so I well remember when the ULM Warhawks were the Northeast Louisiana Indians.**

- **The Tim Brando story is completely true.**

- **I mentioned my real 40th birthday in these thoughts, which was a mistake. A friend of mine, John Edwards, figured out I was the author after putting together this piece of information along with my numerous "47" references.**

- Upon reading the Salma Hayek getting naked reference, one poster wrote that he was knocking off work early to go rent the movie.

- Being removed as president of the home owner's association was inspired by an episode of *Seinfeld*.

José's Thoughts on LSU Chapter Tres

Bowl eligible.

Please excuse José for a moment as he regains his composure.

He is known for wearing his emotions on his sleeve (and has a history of taking off his shirt), so it is not surprising that José wept uncontrollably this past Saturday as the final seconds ticked off the clock. He wept as he thought of seniors such as Michael Oher, Jamarca Sanford, Peria Jerry, and Jason Cook, who persevered and were ultimately rewarded. He wept as he contemplated how different the Ole Miss football program was just one year ago. And finally, José wept when he got back to his tent and discovered that his tequila and Subway sandwiches (which are just $5 for a foot-long in case you were somehow not aware) were missing.

Fortunately for José, he always keeps emergency bottles of tequila hidden in various locales around the Southeastern United States, including forty-seven Oxford locations. After Saturday night, that number was reduced to forty-four. Before you assume that José consumed three bottles of tequila celebrating the 59-0 shellacking of ULM, know that the one he had hidden behind the Jack Kerouac books (the last place he thought anyone would look) at Square Books was missing. So if you happened to run into an intoxicated person wearing a beret over the weekend, chances are that's the dude that stole José's tequila.

On to LSU.

José does not like LSU for many reasons. Besides the fact that they ruined corndog consumption for all decent people, they are generally an obnoxious, swarthy bunch. *Note: José used to partake of the occasional corn dog (especially at the fair), but since they have become so identified with fans of LSU, he can no longer enjoy them for fear of somehow being identified with Tiger fans.*

LSU fans and athletes alike also lack the common sense and decency that is present in those of most every other school (Alabama and The School Whose Name Shall Not be Spoken excepted). This was never more evident than when Ronald Reagan was shot shortly after assuming the office of President of the United States in 1981. This incident happened just before the NCAA Basketball Final Four, which LSU was participating in that year. There was discussion at the time that perhaps the Final Four should be cancelled. Some of the players set to play were asked about such a possibility. Their responses:

Virginia center, Ralph Sampson: "This is a time of great pain for our country and at such a time basketball is not the highest priority."

North Carolina guard, Jimmy Black: "My thoughts and prayers are with the President, and while I want to play, I will support whatever decision is made."

Indiana forward, Ray Tolbert: "Is cancelling the Final Four the correct response? I cannot answer that question. All I know is that I, along with every other American citizen, am heartbroken about this incident."

LSU center, Leonard Mitchell: "Lots of people gets shot lots of times. But they ain't never cancelled no basketball game."

Ok. José must admit that he made up one of those quotes. The sad part is that it was not the Leonard Mitchell one.

A few people have inquired as to whether José will attend the game in Baton Rouge. Unfortunately he will not. He has been to five Ole Miss-LSU matchups in Tiger Stadium, and the Rebels have a 3-2 record in his visits there, so his reasons for not going are in no way related to his fear of the outcome, or of the treatment he might receive from the fans of Louisiana State. No, his primary concern is that his pastor recently warned José about his continued fraternization with sinners and one might readily assume that there will not be a greater collection of sinners in a more confined location anywhere on earth than there will be at Tiger Stadium Saturday night. *Note: Before any of the more theologically astute out there responds, "But we are all sinners José," he is completely aware of that. LSU fans just seem to be a little better at it than everyone else.*

Speaking of his pastor, José's must admit he sometimes gets mixed signals from him. While he does seem concerned about José's eternal fate, he has on more than one occasion commented, "Have you ever thought about giving the Baptist church a try?" In fact José has contemplated the Immersionists. There is no question that Baptist women are better cooks than their Presbyterians counterparts, and José has crashed more than one Baptist funeral for the after-service food. On the other hand, you can never be sure when a Baptist worship service is going to end. When a Presbyterian minister wraps up his sermon, you've got two to three minutes tops before you will be able to head for the exit. With Baptists, there's always the possibility that a few people will decide they need to get saved and if that happens you can abandon all hope of seeing the first quarter of the Saints game. These are the kinds of things that must be considered before deciding on a particular denomination. Of course for a small percentage of people, doctrinal issues might also come into play.

But José digresses. Back to LSU.

The game this weekend is huge. Since there is no longer a doubt that the Rebels will be bowling, the question now is where? Most of the prognostications José has seen have the team going to the Liberty, Music City, Peach or Cotton Bowl. Wins the next two weeks would make the Cotton Bowl the most likely destination. This excites José as he had a great time there in 2004. Plus José just plain likes cotton. Approximately 20% of his wardrobe is comprised of cotton products (The remaining 80% comes from polyester, terrycloth, and velour).

José will not make a prediction on the result of the game this weekend. He can tell you that he is certain that Coach Nutt's boys will not go to Baton Rouge hoping that they can win, or thinking that they can win. They will go expecting to win.

My name is José Valdez IV and these are my thoughts.

Notes:

- **I believe they have been airing the Subway "five dollar foot long" commercial 1,000 times daily. I am personally boycotting the place until they cease and desist.**

- **I probably do consume fewer corndogs annually because of LSU.**

- **I had heard the Leonard Mitchell quote years ago, but thought that Rudy Macklin or Dewayne Scales said it. I went to my source for all Ole Miss sports related answers, Jody Varner, to get the correct player.**

- The "fraternizing with sinners" comment was inspired by a quote from the pulpit of First Presbyterian Church in Jackson. I know I shouldn't be seeking material during the Sunday sermons but I couldn't help it on this one.

- Even though I am Presbyterian, I do want the Baptists to handle the food at my funeral.

José's Thoughts on The School Whose Name Shall Not be Spoken Chapter Tres

Ole Miss is better than LSU.

It was impossible to watch the game this past Saturday and come to any other conclusion. The Rebels were better at every position on the field. Ole Miss coaches were sharper than their Tiger counterparts. The ball boys were quicker. The trainers and managers were superior. Rebel fans were louder and as is always the case; the Ole Miss women were better looking. It was complete and utter domination in every category.

It was just a great week all around. The coaches designed a wonderful game-plan. The players had a fine week of practice. Transportation to Baton Rouge went smoothly (Wait. Scratch that one). The Rebels showed up ready to play and executed brilliantly on the field. It was a beautiful thing to behold. One might say it was Salma Hayekesque.

As he is sure was the case with most of you, José's reaction to this was to consume more tequila than was necessary and begin text messaging ex-girlfriends who are currently incarcerated to see if he could be added to their conjugal visit list. *Note: Two of the seven responses he received were favorable.*

But that was last week, and this is Egg Bowl week so José must focus his attention on The School Whose Name Shall Not be Spoken (TSWNSNBS).

José has spent a considerable amount of time (not as much as time as he has spent working on his ice sculpture of Ricardo Montalban, but still considerable) contemplating who the most valuable player for Ole Miss football of the past year should be and has come to the conclusion that one player stands above all the others in his contribution to the success of the 2008 Rebel football squad. That person is ... Derek Pegues. Yes, were it not for a huge punt return in last years Egg Bowl game by Mr. Pegues, Houston Nutt would not be at Ole Miss and it is highly unlikely that bowl scenarios would be the topic of conversation among Rebel fans. Now, José does not like to lose to TSWNSNBS, but can easily see that doing so last year was the best thing that has happened to the Ole Miss program in quite some time. In fact, should the next five to ten years of Rebel football go as well as José believes they could, he will be passing around the sombrero asking for donations for a Pegues statue to go outside of Vaught-Hemingway. So as you enjoy your Thanksgiving meal this Thursday, be sure and give thanks for Derek Pegues and all he has done for Ole Miss football.

While on the subject of Pegues, some supporter of TSWNSNBS decided it would be hilarious to put a billboard with a picture of his punt return against Ole Miss last year with the words "Many Happy Returns" on it, close to the Batesville exit on I-55, so all Rebel fans would see it and be reminded of that day. Well, he was correct about it being humorous because Jorge, Paco and José laugh like a pack of hyenas until tequila shoots out of their nostrils every time they see it. What fans of the TSWNSNBS considered their greatest day in many years has turned into their worst nightmare. Perhaps you have heard the term "instant gratification". Well there is no better example of the pitfalls of it (other than the date with the crazy Delta Gamma José had in college that has led to a 20-year *Fatal Attraction* scenario. Were it not for his love of Rebel athletics, José would have long ago relocated to Nepal to seek work as a Sherpa). Hopefully TSWNSNBS spends the next 20 years suffering the consequences of their brief moment in the sun.

On a subject of much importance that he has not previously addressed, José feels the time is now right. It regards cowbells. There is a ban on cowbells at SEC stadiums that many people feel should be strictly enforced. José is firmly in the camp that disagrees. He encourages fans of TSWNSNBS to bring their cowbells to the game this Friday. In fact, José believes not only that there should not be a ban, but that indeed there should be a law that requires all fans of TSWNSNBS to carry a cowbell with them at all times. It would be quite beneficial to the public at large to be able to identify these people on those rare occasions when they are not adorned in maroon sweat suits. They should also have cowbells as hood ornaments on their vehicles, cowbells at their front doors to signal when city folk have arrived, and cowbells residing on their bedside tables to alert their significant other that they are ready to mate.

As for the game this Friday, it is going to be a thrashing. While José can look back and laugh about last season's contest, he can guarantee that the Ole Miss football team does not share the same feelings. They want to make it clear that those days are gone and a new one is dawning.

"FOR THE LOVE OF GOD, NO!" You say. "You know what happens when you go into a game expecting victory José!"

That is the past. José has made it clear that he reserves the right to change his approach should the Rebels win a few important football games. Well they have. This is not José IV's Rebels. This is a new generation of Rebels; José V's generation. José is just happy that he can enjoy watching them. Besides, Coach Nutt expects to win. The team expects to win. Why should José not follow suit?

So to the fans of TSWNSNBS, José says bring your cowbells. Ring them early though, because there will not be many occasions to do so as the day progresses. And as long as Houston Nutt is the coach of the Ole Miss football team, these opportunities will be few and far between. So as you ring your cattle percussion instruments this Friday, ask not for whom the cowbell tolls. It tolls for thee.

My name is José Valdez IV and these are my thoughts.

Notes:

- My comment on the transportation to Baton Rouge was in reference to the big topic of discussion on the message boards that week concerning the fact that the team was bussing to Baton Rouge rather than flying.

- I cannot account as to the whereabouts of all of my ex-girlfriends, but to my knowledge, none of them are currently incarcerated.

- The Pegues billboard is still up as of May 2009. It remains hilarious.

- My prediction of a thrashing proved to be accurate. The final score was 45-0 and it was as complete a domination as I've ever seen from a Rebel team.

Jose's Thoughts on the Egg Bowl

José must apologize for the delay in sharing his thoughts about the recent performance of the Rebels in the Egg Bowl. He has been distracted, alternately spending time on Facebook sending friend requests to various Ole Miss sorority house mothers and working on his novel. It is a historical fiction account of what the ramifications might have been had Ruth Bader Ginsburg not been confirmed as a Supreme Court Justice. We're talking human sacrifice. Dogs and cats living together. Mass hysteria. José believes this book could take the market by storm since no one else has addressed this possibility.

José decided to experiment with something new for the Egg Bowl this past week. Sobriety. Now tequila has served José well for Ole Miss games in recent years because the memory loss comes in quite handy on most occasions. Going into this game however, José determined that he would like to remember every play, so he was sans tequila. This proved to be an excellent decision because he got to witness the game with all of his faculties intact. As for after the game, suffice it to say that he is now down to thirty-nine Oxford locations where he has bottles of tequila hidden.

The game this past weekend ranks among the most decisive beatdowns in all of history. Negative fifty-one yards rushing? Thirty-seven yards total offense? Are you kidding José? As he is sure was the case with most of you, José could not help but be reminded of some of the great military disasters in history. These include:

- Agincourt- Henry V leads British forces to victory against a French contingent that outnumbers his group by at least a 3-1 margin and perhaps as much as 10-1. The French that are not killed or captured run like a bunch of sissies.

- Waterloo- Napoleon leads French forces against those of the Seventh Coalition (U.K., Russia, Austria, Prussia, and some other guys) in Belgium. The French defeat is decisive and marks the end of Napoleon's military career. The School Whose Name Shall Not be Spoken is pretty much the France of the SEC.

- Little Big Horn- Custer assumes there are approximately 800 Cheyenne in the area. The number was more like 1,800. This may well have been where the phrase "You know what happens when you assume" got its start.

- Balaclava- Known for the famous Charge of the Light Brigade; Lord Cardigan leads British cavalry troops to the slaughter against a Russian force armed with heavy artillery. One can't help but think that had Derek Pegues been a British cavalry officer at this time, his horse would have conveniently pulled a hamstring before he got within cannon range.

- Santa Poco- El Guapo, Jefe, and their band of marauders are routed by the people of Santa Poco and three American actors.

Many have mentioned that Ole Miss should put up some kind of billboard outside of Starkville to answer the "Many Happy Returns" one that TSWNSNBS displayed near the Batesville exit after last year's game. Jorge suggested a picture of Peria Jerry with the slogan "Stepped onto the Maroon." Paco preferred going somewhat understated, no picture, just "45-0. Suck it." José believes Ole Miss should stay classy and that a billboard is not necessary. When you come into contact with fans of TSWNSNBS, just give them the nod. Words aren't necessary. They'll understand.

As for Coach Croom losing his job, of course José was disappointed about this. It will be virtually impossible for them not to upgrade their coaching situation. This is indeed a critical hire for TSWNSNBS as it could mean the difference between losing the next ten meetings with the Rebels, or only eight of them.

Fans of TSWNSNBS can take some solace in the fact that Peria Jerry will not be back next year. Unfortunately for them, most of the other ten guys that they couldn't block are returning. With the talent they have currently assembled on their roster José suggests that the slogan for TSWNSNBS should be "Wait until 2013!"

All José has to do now is sit back and wait to see which bowl game the Rebs go to. It is not a matter of great concern to him as both Orlando and Dallas have tequila, loose women, and rollercoasters.

My name is José Valdez IV and these are my thoughts.

Notes:

- The "human sacrifice…dogs and cats living together" reference is from *Ghostbusters.*
- The Santa Poco reference is from *Three Amigos.*
- The "stay classy" reference comes from *Anchorman.*

José's Thoughts on Madrid

Madrid died.

For those unfamiliar, Madrid was José's dog (He names all of his dogs after Mexican Presidents). It was time for him to go, but still difficult nonetheless. Madrid was more faithful than any of José's three wives and less judgmental than the choir members at his church. He was also a good judge of character as he refused to make eye contact with The Wife Whose Name Shall Not be Spoken or even acknowledge her presence.

Now José could never discern how big an Ole Miss fan Madrid was because he typically left the room whenever the Rebels were on television. It is entirely possible that he did so because José was prone to yell profanities at the top of his lungs during Ole Miss contests, and not because he didn't love the Rebels. In fact, on one of Madrid's final days he stayed in front of the television for the entire Ole Miss-LSU game. José must remember to send a thank you note to Coach Nutt for sending him out a winner. (Right after he sends one that reads "Sign Andrew Ritter!").

Madrid did more than his share of structural damage to various domiciles over the course of his life. And there is no question that armadillos throughout the Southeast are celebrating his demise, as Madrid took out quite a few when he was in his prime. José will not make the claim that Madrid was the greatest dog in the world, but he was a damn good one. Willie Morris would have liked him. In fact José was reading the copy of *My Dog Skip* that Willie signed for José V on his first birthday to Madrid near the end.

José has heard it said that all dogs go to heaven. Since, despite José's protestations, the Presbyterian Church has chosen not to take a doctrinal stance on this issue, he is not sure if that is correct. He can say though that he has met a few dogs in his day that he would prefer Madrid not have to spend eternity with, including the one that is currently yapping on the back porch of José's next door neighbor.

José is not sharing his thoughts on Madrid to gain sympathy. There will be plenty of other occasions when he needs that. His primary motivation for these thoughts is that they be a tribute to Madrid the Great. Also, after a period of mourning and tequila consumption, José is interested in getting another dog. So if you know of someone with lab puppies that are not likely to get bigger than 80 lbs (this may be José's last dog) and they are no further north than Oxford, south than Hattiesburg, west than Vicksburg or east than Meridian send José a message to his inbox. Oh, it would also be helpful if the dog looks like it could be named Tejada or Camacho.

My name is José Valdez IV and these are my thoughts.

Notes:

- **Truman (Madrid) died early Thanksgiving morning.**
- **He always got up and left the room after I started yelling at the television, but did hang in there for the LSU game.**
- **Coach Nutt did sign Andrew Ritter.**
- **Truman took out a number of armadillos while we lived in Tampa.**
- **Willie Morris signed a copy of *My Dog Skip* at Square Books for my oldest son Will on his first birthday. A few years later we saw Willie at The Mayflower in Jackson. He commented on what a fine looking boy he was and asked his name. When my wife told him it was Will, he said we should call him Willie.**
- **My last paragraph was sincere and I did receive a few responses about potential dogs. We ended up adopting a three year-old yellow lab that we named Scout. We just didn't think he looked presidential. He's not as smart as Truman (at least not yet) but we love him anyway.**

José's Thoughts on the Kennedy Situation

This is all José's fault.

After months of stalking the coach, when Kennedy needed José the most, he wasn't there. Had José kept his normal routine of following Kennedy's every move, he might have been able to step us as a witness and refute these accusations. But alas, José was not present in Cincinnati due to a previous obligation José had involving wealthy divorcées in Northeast Jackson.

As you can imagine, José has been much chagrined over the allegations involving Coach Kennedy made by TCDWNJCP (The Cab Driver Whose Name José Cannot Pronounce). José hasn't felt this low since his unsuccessful persistent attempts to convince the band The White Animals that adding a keytar player of Latino descent would bring in more chicks. What has brought him the most consternation though is that he let Coach Kennedy down. Now in all fairness, it must be acknowledged that even had José been present, he might not have been able to do much good for Coach Kennedy, as José is not generally accepted as a credible witness, due to various factors which are neither here nor there.

As for what actually happened that night, José cannot be certain. However, everyone is well aware that on the general trustworthiness scale, cab drivers rank just above Bobby Petrino and only below valet parking attendants (José saw *Ferris Bueller's Day Off*). Besides being untrustworthy, cab drivers are known provokers. If José had been arrested for every incident involving a cab driver, well...he would have been arrested more times than he actually has been.

José is prepared to sit back and see how things shake out. If anyone is aware of how easily one can be falsely accused of something, it is José. The list of things he has been accused of over the years is a long one and includes, but is not limited to the following:

- Starting the fire that burned down The Warehouse.
- Taking six hours a semester his final year of school in order to see all of Gerald Glass' senior season.
- Dating Kathy Manning in college.
- Parting his hair on the side for a brief period in an attempt to be more "socially acceptable".
- Instigating the 1985 Derby Day brawl between the Kappa's and Phi Mu's.
- Accepting money to throw the 1989 intramural flag football championship.
- Taking a date to see *Beaches*.
- Purchasing a Frankie Goes to Hollywood cassette tape.
- Feigning interest in the work of Fyodor Dostoevsky in order to attract the attention of a certain English graduate student.
- Smoking clove cigarettes.

Note: Since José's "counselor" has suggested that his life might improve were he to be more honest, José must admit that no one has ever really accused him of dating Kathy Manning, and that approximately half of the above accusations are accurate.

José has to believe that Coach Kennedy will be exonerated. He does not want to live in world where Kennedy is not the coach of the Ole Miss basketball team; just as he does not want to live in a world where accepting money to go on dates with wealthy divorcées is deemed inappropriate.

My name is José Valdez IV and these are my thoughts.

Notes:

- **I hesitated about writing any thoughts on this topic because there wasn't much humor in the subject. Eventually I decided that lightening the rhetoric on the matter might be beneficial.**

- I have had an incident with a cab driver who tried to drive me in a circuitous route to my hotel in Minneapolis. I refused to pay him the full fare and the police were not involved.

- As previously mentioned, I did indeed take only six hours a semester my final year of graduate school in order to see Gerald Glass play.

- I didn't throw the 1989 intramural flag football championship but there was a pass in the first half that I probably should have caught but didn't. It still haunts me.

- There was no Derby Day brawl between the Kappa's and Phi Mu's in 1985, but there could have been.

- I did own a Frankie Goes to Hollywood tape and am not proud of that fact.

José's Thoughts on Texas Tech

Thirteen months ago the odds that Ole Miss would be playing in the January 2009 Cotton Bowl were about as great as those that José would finally fulfill his lifelong dream of becoming a world-renowned hand model. Since the former has come to fruition, José plans to check into some laser hair-removal options and revive his quest for the latter.

This will be the twelfth bowl game the Rebels have played since José started following Ole Miss football in the mid 1970's. In exactly half of those bowl games the opponent has been either Air Force or Texas Tech. In fact, including the upcoming Cotton Bowl, Ole Miss has played Texas Tech as many times (4) since 1998 as it has played Kentucky, South Carolina and Florida, and twice more than it has played Tennessee. In other words, José is tired of Texas Tech. But he is not one to complain about playing in a bowl game, much less a traditional New Year's Day bowl game.

Many fans in José's age bracket will recall that Ole Miss once had a football coach who came from Texas Tech. His name was Steve Sloan and he was going to restore Rebel football to the heights it had achieved under Johnny Vaught. Excitement was in the air when Sloan arrived and every Ole Miss fan purchased a copy of his book *A Whole New Ballgame.* Well it was a whole new ballgame alright. And it was friggin' horrible. Sloan was an unmitigated disaster. We're talking Orgeron level disaster (without the decent recruiting). One of José's ex mother-in-laws speculated that Sloan was actually listening to the Grand Ole Opry on his headset during the games and there was not much that happened on the field during those years that would dispute such an assertion. In the five years he served as the head coach, Sloan's record was 20-34-1. Among the Ole Miss coaches whose tenure lasted at least two seasons, only Fred Robbins (whose signature win was a 61-0 shellacking of Hendrix College and whose fate was sealed when he lost the 1916 season finale to Mississippi College 36-14) and the aforementioned Ed Orgeron had lower winning percentages than Sloan. Had José been of legal drinking age during the Sloan years things may have gotten ugly.

But that's all water under the bridge and provided Texas Tech never sends Ole Miss another coach, we're cool.

Chances are that not many of you have visited Lubbock, Texas. José has had the privilege of doing so. Some might argue that Lubbock is the Starkville of the Big Twelve, but José would beg to differ. As long as Ames, Iowa and Manhattan, Kansas are still home to Big Twelve schools, then Lubbock is safe from that comparison. Plus, from the pictures on the internet José has seen, unlike The School Whose Name Shall Not be Spoken, they have a plethora of babes at Texas Tech. Who knew? Now José recognizes that it is entirely possible that these young ladies might not be from Texas Tech and some computer genius may have photo-shopped Red Raider t-shirts (very small, very tight Red Raider t-shirts mind you) onto the bodies of Florida State coeds, but he is going to give them the benefit of the doubt. José fully intends to spend his time between now and the Cotton Bowl sending Facebook friend requests to various young ladies in the Lubbock vicinity, since the ones he sends to Ole Miss coeds are rejected on a regular basis.

On another positive note, Lubbock was the hometown of Buddy Holly. Older Rebel fans remember Holly as one of the pioneers of rock and roll who recorded such hits as "That'll Be the Day" and "Peggy Sue". When middle-aged Rebel fans think of him they recall *The Buddy Holly Story* with Gary Busey, or perhaps *La Bamba,* where Holly was one of the artists who also tragically died in the plane crash that killed Richie Valens (portrayed by Lou Diamond Phillips at the apex of his career). Younger Rebel fans know him as a guy Weezer had a song about.

Texas Tech is coached by Mike Leach and he's not bad. Leach went to BYU and is apparently a Mormon, which means he doesn't drink tequila. José III says Mormons don't go to heaven, but of course José III also believes the Baptists, Methodists, Catholics, Seventh Day Adventists, Pentecostals and pretty much anyone who isn't Presbyterian won't be in heaven either, so you can take that for what it's worth. José IV is much more inclusive, believing he'll see many denominations, other than the Methodists, represented in heaven someday.

Red Raider fans can look forward to Leach spending many years at their school, unless by chance, he is offered the head coaching job at most any SEC, Big Ten, ACC, Pac 10, or Arena Football League team in the near future. If you are not a native Lubbockonian (or is it Lubbockite?), there are only so many times you can stomach visiting the cow chip house at the National Ranching Heritage Center, and Leach has likely reached his limit.

Jorge, Paco and José are heading to Dallas very soon. New Year's Eve will of course be spent at Six Flags, where they have numerous rollercoasters. You know how much José likes rollercoasters. Unfortunately according to the Six Flags website, their best rollercoaster, the Batman one, is temporarily closed. This is extremely disappointing to José. Unless Six Flags is prepared to handle a Clark W. Griswold at Wally World type incident, he suggests they get it up and running immediately.

As for the actual game, it should be exciting. José cannot tell you everything that will happen, but he is confident that many of the below will occur:

- That Texas Tech lineman who paints his face will frighten a few small children.

- During the first quarter there will be at least five posts by Ole Miss fans watching at home commenting on how biased the announcers are towards Texas Tech.

- After the first questionable call by an official, Jorge will yell his obligatory "If you had another eye you'd be a Cyclops" insult.

- Numerous Texas Tech fans will comment on how hot Ole Miss girls are.

- There will be an argument on the Texas Tech sideline among coaches and players concerning who is supposed to be blocking Peria Jerry.

- José will say something inappropriate to a woman seated near him who turns out to be married to someone much larger than José.

- Coach Nutt will get excited and do that signal where he flaps his arms like a bird that is unable to fly (perhaps an ostrich).

- José will receive a text message from his pastor sometime during the third quarter asking if he has been drinking again. (José will lie).

- Jevan Sneed will throw for 280 yards.

- The Rebels will rush for 350 yards.

- Rebels win 38-30.

My name is José Valdez IV and these are my thoughts.

Notes:

- Someone posted these thoughts on the Texas Tech board and they were removed within five minutes. They're apparently an overly sensitive bunch.

- The hand model reference comes from an episode of *Seinfeld*.

- My mother-in-law did make the comment about Steve Sloan listening to The Grand Ole Opry on his headset during games.

- There were pictures circulating on the internet of Texas Tech coeds around this time and they were quite attractive. Not Ole Miss level attractive, but attractive nonetheless.

- Weezer has a song "Buddy Holly".

- My father (Jose III) actually is, and always has been, Baptist (but he's a closet Presbyterian).

- My predictions for the game proved to be fairly accurate.

José's Thoughts on the Cotton Bowl

José's quest to Dallas for the Cotton Bowl had an inauspicious beginning. As he previously stated, there were reports that the Batman rollercoaster at Six Flags would not be in operation. Well they were accurate. Not only that, but the Texas Giant was also not running due to the "cold weather". Close one great rollercoaster and there's a possibility that José will not make a spectacle of himself. Close two of them and all bets are off.

Then on New Year's morning José awakened to discover he had forgotten to pack his razor. This forced him to use one of the complimentary ones provided by his hotel, which was apparently made in an Indonesian juvenile sweat shop, because he was rendered virtually unrecognizable by it. You can imagine the blistering commentary card he left for the hotel staff. Surely it will put an end to their stocking of such an inferior product (and perhaps, as an added bonus, lead to a decline in Indonesian juvenile sweat shops as well).

Things began to look up for José on the day of the game. Determined that they would not make the same mistake they did in 2004, Jorge, Paco, and José left their hotel four hours before game time. They were the first ones to enter the parking lot, and made sure to park at the very back, so at the end of the day, if necessary, they could be the first ones to leave. Of course José put on his headphones, turned on his iPod, cued up "Chariots of Fire" and sprinted to the gates.

Since the gates were not yet open, José was forced to mingle with some of the Texas Tech fans. All were confident of victory and spoke about the plans they had for that evening's celebratory hootenanny. José did notice quite a few people staring at him and figured it was due to either the results of the shaving incident or perhaps they were admiring the Ole Miss sweater vest he had been given as a gift for Christmas. As it turns out, it likely was the latter. Paco waited until the second quarter to inform José that the generally accepted practice was to wear some type of garment underneath the sweater vest such as a button down or polo shirt. Even mock turtlenecks or t-shirts are sometimes deemed appropriate. Apparently wearing only a sweater vest is frowned upon.

But José digresses. On to the Cotton Bowl.

The mindset has changed. Being a fan of Ole Miss football doesn't mean what it did for pretty much all of José's life prior to this point. From the time he started following the Rebels, up until a few weeks ago, a 14-0 deficit to an 8th ranked team (or just about any team) would have crushed José's spirit and he would have vowed they had no chance. José didn't feel that way at the Cotton Bowl. Rather than being despondent, he was just a little ticked off. Now he cannot say that at that point he knew they would come back, but he did know they were perfectly capable of doing so. And that is exactly what is different about being an Ole Miss football fan for José these days.

José did gain confidence after the first Rebel touchdown though, because it was at that point that he first noticed the Texas Tech bell-ringer. You see, teams that ring bells don't have success against this Ole Miss football team.

Once the Rebels tied the game at 14-14 it was over. Even though the Red Raiders would take another lead at 21-14, you knew, José knew, the American people knew that the Rebs were not going to be denied the Cotton Bowl trophy. As José surveyed the field it occurred to him that there were no more than four or five guys on Texas Tech's roster who could start for Ole Miss (and Graham Harrell ain't one of them). The Rebels clearly had the superior talent. So José doesn't want to hear any more crapola about the Big Twelve, and specifically the Big Twelve South. The SEC does have some defenses that are comparable to Big Twelve defenses. They're called scout teams (and that is likely an insult to most SEC scout teams).

It was a fantastic day to be in Dallas and an even better day to be an Ole Miss Rebel. After celebrating more than was absolutely necessary, Jorge, Paco and José made their way to the team hotel. A quick $20 payoff led them to Houston Nutt's room where they stood outside and serenaded the Coach with their rendition of "Everybody Have Fun Tonight". Coach Nutt came outside to see what the hell was going on, but was still on such a high he joined in on the singing, providing the "Everybody Wang Chung tonight" portions of the song. However when José asked if they could follow up with "Under Pressure" (Jorge provides the beat-box sound, Paco does a mean David Bowie, and José can nail the Freddie Mercury falsetto.) Coach Nutt declined. Maybe next time.

It was an amazing season. José can typically judge what kind of year it was by how many games remain on his TIVO at the end of the year. Right now he still has the Florida, Arkansas, Auburn, LSU, Mississippi State and Texas Tech games on his list. This is far more than he has had the prior five years combined (by about six). He intends to watch them all repeatedly in between viewings of *Lawrence of Arabia.* (He was an English guy. He came to fight the Turkish). So it is with great pride, but a bit of sadness that José bids adieu to the 2008 Ole Miss football team; possibly the best, certainly the most fun group since he began following Rebel football in 1977.

Oct 10, 2009: Ole Miss vs. Alabama. José's birthday. ESPN Gameday in the Grove. Book it.

My name is José Valdez IV and these are my thoughts.

Notes:

- **My friend, Sam Hubbard, my boys and I, did go to Six Flags a couple of days before the game and the rollercoasters I mentioned were indeed closed.**

- **I truly did forget to pack my razor for the trip and had to use a complimentary one provided by the hotel. I lost quite a bit of blood.**

- **We did leave the hotel to go to the game much earlier than in 2004 and the "first ones in the parking lot" reference is from *Vacation.***

- **I wore a sweater vest to the game (with a shirt). After posting these thoughts, a poster on the Ole Miss Spirit message board, Rocky Miskelly, added a picture of two Mexican wrestlers. He had photo-shopped a red Ole Miss sweater vest onto one of them. I liked it so much that I made it my profile picture on FaceBook.**

- **The "English guy. Came to fight the Turkish" reference is from *Hollywood Knights*.**

- **Hopefully by the time this book comes out, my prediction about ESPN Gameday coming to Oxford on October 10 will be a reality.**

José's Thoughts

It has been almost three weeks since the glorious Cotton Bowl victory over Texas Tech from TMOCOAT (The most overrated conference of all-time) and yet José is still on an emotional high. He has watched the game on his Tivo multiple times now. Yet because of the less than enthusiastic broadcast, as José is certain is the case with most of you, he now watches with the sound turned down while listening to Christopher Cross' Greatest Hits Live. *Note: You really haven't experienced the game until you have seen Marshay's interception return with "Arthur's Theme" as the background music.* Were he given a choice, José would prefer to hibernate from now until the 2009 football season kicks off in Memphis on September 5, perhaps awakening just briefly on national signing day to see if the Rebels landed Bobby Massie. Sadly, until Hybernol becomes a reality, that is not an option.

Fortunately, José is likely to be entertained between now and then just reading the comments that the new coach from The School Whose Name Shall Not be Spoken offers his subjects. José does not blame him at all for such pontificating though. What should he tell them? "Look people, I just pray that I can deliver one winning season so I can get out of this hell hole as soon as possible." Honestly Mullen had no idea what he was getting into. José is quite certain that immediately after he was hired, upon exiting the plane at the Golden Triangle Regional Airport and being serenaded by a cacophony of cowbell ringing, he had a Ron Burgundy in the bear pit "I immediately regret this decision!" moment. You know in your heart of hearts that is the truth.

José would be remiss if he did not address the current state of Ole Miss basketball. To say that it has been a frustrating season would not do it justice. Considering the legal issues facing Coach Kennedy and the injuries the team has sustained it would be easy to just write this season off. José chooses to be patient though. Someone once said "I believe that man will not only endure, he will prevail." (José cannot recall exactly who said that, but it was someone very famous, like Cuba Gooding Jr.). Well, perhaps not this season, but somewhere down the road; José believes the young men on this basketball team will prevail.

Still, there is no getting around the fact that the Rebels must complete the current schedule. Everyone should agree by now that expectations must be lowered. This should not be too difficult a problem for José as he has vast experience with lowering his expectations. From a Toyota Celica Supra to a Chrysler K car; from a job in the pharmaceutical industry to an entry level position at an asbestos factory; from Susan Akin to "Cindy" the foul-mouthed, chain-smoking, bipolar, Kappa Delta (actually that wasn't such a bad three weeks); José has managed to live with things that were not what he had originally hoped for. He can do it again.

José has on many prior occasions let his feelings be known about tomorrow night's basketball opponent; the University of Alabama. He doesn't care for them at all. Indeed, he doesn't care for the entire state of Alabama and refuses to even acknowledge it with his presence. This proves inconvenient when traveling from Yocona to the Flora-Bama Lounge (the entire bar is actually in Florida), but a man must have his principles. No matter the outcome of the basketball contest, it will not impact José's preparation for the Crimson Tide coming to town October 10, in what may be the biggest football game of his lifetime. José is already seeking additional tequila stashing locations in the Oxford area and is actively searching Facebook for a date that weekend. *Note: Said date need not attend the actual game, in fact José encourages her not to. She just needs to be available for other weekend "festivities".*

Fifteen days until National Signing Day.

My name is José Valdez IV and these are my thoughts.

Notes:

- **The Rebels did land Bobbie Massie, my number one target.**
- **The Hybernol reference comes from a *Saturday Night Live* skit with Chris Farley.**
- **The "Ron Burgundy in the bear pit" is a reference to *Anchorman*.**

- Of course the "I believe man will not only endure, he will prevail." quote is from Faulkner. Even I went to the library enough in college to know that.

- I wanted a Supra in college and ended up with a K car; a car so boring I referred to it as the twin turbo K.

José's (Painfully Long) Thoughts on the 2009 Recruiting Class Part One

José has previously alluded to the fact that his mindset as a Rebel fan had changed thanks to Houston Nutt. He no longer goes into big games expecting disastrous things to happen and that has carried over into recruiting. Signing day was typically a day of shattered dreams (Frank Gore, Joe McKnight, etc.) for Rebel fans and one which José always approached with fear and trepidation. Not this signing day. This time José awakened with a sense of hope and anticipation.

As a general rule of thumb, José does not begin consuming tequila before 10:00 A.M. on weekdays. When Patrick Patterson announced he would attend Ole Miss at approximately 9:13 A.M. this past Wednesday, all of a sudden that seemed like a ridiculous way to go through life. José also typically eschews drinking scotch before noon, but when Bobbie Massie chose the Rebels over Alabama at 10:17 A.M. that restraint also seemed frivolous. By 1:30 P.M. when Tim Simon, Jamar Hornsby and Raymond Cotton were all safely in the fold, José had violated every sanction on drinking, trash talking, and public nudity he had imposed upon himself. Had he only been able to top it all off with some potato logs from The Chevron and a hot fudge brownie from The Hoka, it might have been the greatest day of his life.

It has taken quite some time for José to collect himself after National Signing Day; a day that will live in infamy for the Rebel faithful. He is not one prone to boastfulness, but José believes Ole Miss put together the pieces necessary for global domination the next few years. Just as The School Whose Name Shall Not be Spoken had reason for a small semblance of hope, they watched one big name after another commit to the Rebs, beginning the weekend before signing day and culminating with those who waited to make it official this past Wednesday.

José fully recognizes that he is like most Rebel fans and upon reading the biographies of the signees, immediately ponders which historical figures are brought to mind by each of them. Now José was not prepared for Houston Nutt to sign 38 players so he has chosen to break his thoughts into three parts, with parts two and three coming in subsequent weeks. Otherwise his thoughts this week would be approximately ten pages. Even breaking them into three parts, they are obnoxiously long and José recommends you do not read them if you are driving, easily bored, or prone to narcolepsy. The players profiled this week and the following weeks are in no particular order and are paired with the historical figure that comes to mind with each of them. Most of these are rather obvious and your list is likely very similar to José's.

Bobbie Massie- Arthur, King of the Britons

King Arthur was the legendary medieval British leader whose very existence has been hotly debated. He is purported to have proven himself the rightful king by pulling the sword from the stone. Along with his noble knights of the round table, he defended Britain against attacks by Saxon invaders and established Camelot.

Much like Arthur, Bobbie Massie has done legendary things and performed fantastic feats of strength. But because José has not witnessed these exploits in person he doubts their veracity and questions whether Massie truly exists either. No one can possibly be the beast that Bobbie Massie is suggested to be. However, if reports are accurate, José must soon begin composing an epic in his honor.

Tig Barksdale- William of Ockham

William of Ockham was a 14ᵗʰ Century English Franciscan Friar and philosopher. He is best remembered for establishing Occam's Razor, which is the principle that states that the explanation of any phenomenon should make as few assumptions as possible, eliminating those that make no difference in the observable predictions in the explanatory hypothesis or theory. In other words, stick with the simplest explanation. José thinks of Occam's Razor when he hears leaves rustling outside his window at night and it helps him believe that it is probably just the wind and not El Chupacabra coming to get him.

Assuming that Barksdale winds up in the defensive secondary (and that is not a given), Occam's Razor will come into play. If you are a wide-receiver running across the middle and feel like you have been hit by a freight train, it is more likely that you have just been introduced to Tig Barksdale.

Corey Gaines – Leonard Smalls

Leonard Smalls, the motorcycle riding "warthog from hell" cut a wide swath of destruction in the Arizona desert, while causing H.I. McDonough and Nathan Junior much consternation and harming a few innocent creatures in the process.

Expect Corey Gaines, the Army All-American defensive lineman, to terrorize opposing offenses throughout the Southeastern Conference, creating fear not only in them, but also in small children for the foreseeable future.

Evan Swindoll – Miguel de Cervantes

Cervantes, the prominent Spanish novelist, poet and playwright, wrote the classic *Don Quixote* (one of Jose's favorites), which details the misadventures of a would-be knight and his dim-witted neighbor, Sancho Panza. *Don Quixote* is considered by many critics to be the first novel ever written.

Evan Swindoll was a Georgia first team 3A All-State offensive lineman his senior year; prior to that he played at Spain Park High School in Hoover, Alabama.

Tim Simon - Cochise

Cochise was the infamous (it means more than famous) Apache leader who valiantly led his tribe against intrusions by various American contingents in the mid 1800's. He was also imprisoned at one point in his life, but managed to escape.

José cannot confirm that Tim Simon was kidnapped by Clemson supporters shortly before signing day, but many Rebel supporters suspected as much. If this was accurate then Simon also managed an escape. Among those who had previously committed to the Rebs, Simon was the one José was most concerned about on signing day. He is going to be a stud and it is a very good thing that he will be one in a Rebel uniform.

Ja-Mes Logan – Jan-Michael Vincent

Jan-Michael Vincent is perhaps best known to those of José's generation as the star of the movie *The World's Greatest Athlete* or the television program *Air Wolf*. To younger generations he may be best known as the former B-list actor who got in a wreck in Vicksburg last year. He is the first person of prominence with a hyphenated name that José can recall from his childhood.

Ja-Mes Logan has taken the hyphenated name to a new level by actually having the hyphen in the middle of his first name. That alone probably should have been worth another star in the recruiting rankings. José is seriously contemplating changing the spelling of his first name to J-osé (pronounced "huh-ozay") as a tribute to Ja-Mes.

D.T. Shackelford – The Apostle Paul

Now José fully recognizes that when most of you saw that the Rebels had inked D.T. Shackelford you immediately associated him with Ernest Shackleton, the great explorer of the South Pole who was able to rescue all 28 men of the ship Endurance after it was encased in ice, but José chose to go in another direction with The Apostle Paul. Paul, the persecutor of Christians, was blinded by a great light on the road to Damascus, heard the voice of Jesus, converted, and immediately changed his ways.

D.T. Shackelford, the dominating 4-star defensive lineman from Decatur, Alabama, had been a long time Tennessee commitment until he heard the voice of Houston Nutt telling him he was headed down a path that leads to destruction. He chose to follow Nutt and join the Ole Miss squad. Look for Shackelford to be spreading the gospel of Rebel football for a long time to come.

Andrew Ritter – Willie Morris

The author of *North Toward Home, The Courting of Marcus Dupree, Good Ole Boy, My Dog Skip* and many other books, Morris was a Mississippi treasure and great source of pride for many of its residents. He was a Rhodes

Scholar, and although he never attended Ole Miss, he did eventually serve as Writer in Residence on the campus for many years.

Not discounting the fact that Andrew Ritter has one of the strongest legs ever displayed on a high school football field, all reports of him rave about the type of person he is. He is a quality student and someone who should make Rebel fans proud to have him as a representative of their university.

Eric Smiley – Oliver Cromwell

The English Puritan Cromwell was a political and military leader who eventually became Lord Protector of England, Ireland and Scotland. He led the victory over the royalists in the English Civil War and was named as one of the top ten Britons of all-time in a 2002 poll by the BBC.

Eric Smiley, a 6'5" 280lb. defensive lineman from West Helena, Arkansas, looks to wreak havoc among opposing offenses in the near future and was selected one of the top ten players in Arkansas high school football by SuperPrep in 2008.

Korvic Neat – Talleyrand

The French diplomat who worked successfully through the regimes of Louis XVI, Napoleon, Louis XVIII, Charles X, and Louis-Philippe; Talleyrand was extremely instrumental in the formation of the Treaty of Paris after the war between France and the Sixth Coalition, and was able to achieve remarkably lenient terms for France. This was one of many instances that demonstrated his extreme versatility as a diplomat.

Korvic Neat, the Hallandale, Florida star participated in the Under Armor All-American game. He was signed for his versatility and was recruited to some day fill the shoes of Dexter McCluster.

Cameron Whigham – Rod Steiger

Star of over 100 films, Steiger is best known for his Oscar winning performance in the movie *In the Heat of the Night*. He also was featured in the 1996 film *Shiloh;* the story of an abused beagle and the young boy who risks everything to save him.

Cameron Whigham, a 6'3" defensive end from Snellville, Georgia attended Shiloh High School and from early reports, just like José, is a friend of dogs.

Note: If you chose Albert Sydney Johnston, the leader of Confederate troops at the Battle of Shiloh, as the person you associated with Whigham, José completely understands.

Patrick Patterson – Nelson Mandela

Mandela, the South African anti-apartheid activist who spent 27 years in prison and became the first president of his country to be elected in a fully representative democratic election, also won the 1993 Nobel Peace Prize. The dignity he displayed throughout his many ordeals has helped bring people of different races together in South Africa.

Patrick Patterson starred at Noxubee County High School, in the heart of TSWNSNBS territory. He was able to overcome that difficult circumstance, led his team to a state championship, and made the courageous decision to attend Ole Miss. He appears set to catch a plethora of passes from Jevan Snead/Nathan Stanley/Raymond Cotton for the next few years. Ole Miss fans of many races, including at least three Mexicans, will be cheering him on during that time.

My name is José Valdez IV and these are my thoughts.

Notes:
- **I mistakenly named these thoughts Part One rather than Part Uno, as was the José custom.**
- **I still remember exactly where I was when Frank Gore signed with Miami rather than the Rebels; at a Residence Inn outside of Atlanta. That was painful.**
- **There is no telling how many potato logs and hot fudge brownie's I consumed while in school, but it was no more than the amount of Sonic root beer floats and Pizza Den strombolis.**
- **I used "infamy" improperly in this selection and it was pointed out by a poster.**

- The "Arthur, King of the Britons" reference is from *Monty Python and the Holy Grail.*

- Leonard Smalls was the character played by Randall "Tex" Cobb in *Raising Arizona.*

- The "it means more than famous" reference is from *Three Amigos.*

My wife taught Andrew Ritter at Jackson Academy, so we're huge fans and can't wait to see him in a Rebel uniform.

José's Thoughts on the 2009 Recruiting Class Part Dos

José appreciates all of the condolence messages he has received regarding the recent betrothal of Salma Hayek. One person described it as a "dagger to the heart for José." But it is just a flesh wound. If you believe Salma Hayek getting married is going to discourage José from his fifteen year pursuit of her then you do not know José. All he can say to this particular development is "Was it over when the tennis twins bombed Pearl Harbor?" *Note: Ok. José readily admits that was in poor taste. But if you are familiar with the thoughts of José then you are aware that he is not known for exercising good judgment. Indeed, he has quite an impressive record of the exact opposite.*

But José digresses. As he mentioned last week, José is just like most every other Ole Miss fan in that he puts together a list of the signees along with the historical figure that each of them brings to mind. From the feedback he received last week, most fans' lists were very similar to José's. (Although one person said Patrick Patterson made him think of Stephen III of Moldavia, which is just ridiculous).

Below are thirteen more of the 2009 signees with the historical figure they most bring to mind. José apologizes ahead of time for not putting much thought into these. He just went with the first person that came to mind.

Artice Kellum – Stephen III of Moldavia

Stephen III of Moldavia. "Stephen the Great" was the Prince of Moldavia from 1457-1504. During his reign he was able to fight off threats from Hungary, Poland, and the Ottoman Empire, maintaining Moldavia's independence and winning 34 of the 36 battles he fought.

Kellum, the 5'11" 185 lb. safety from Gulliver Prep in Miami who led his team to the Florida 2A State Championship game by winning some tremendous playoff battles, fought off overtures from Tennessee, South Carolina and Minnesota before deciding to cast his lot with the Rebels.

Mike Marry – Alexander Hamilton

Alexander Hamilton was one of the founding fathers and truly one of the more brilliant men in early American history. Hamilton fought in the Revolutionary War, co-wrote the Federalist Papers and was the very first Secretary of the Treasury, where he helped found the U.S. Mint. He is also the dude on $10 bills.

Mike Marry is an extremely bright young man as evidenced by his offer to attend Duke University. He is also quite a football player and one Jose was extremely pleased to sign. He is also the signee most likely to have his likeness eventually appear on some form of currency.

Terrell Grant - Ulysses Everett McGill

Along with his cohorts, Delmar and Pete, McGill roamed the Mississippi Delta countryside, searching for buried loot and hoping to regain the lost love of his life.

Terrell Grant, the Cleveland High receiver has roamed football fields throughout the Mississippi Delta for the past few seasons catching many passes. He could have a very successful career at Ole Miss should he be able to elude the call of beautiful Ole Miss sirens and scurrilous Bible salesmen.

Raymond Cotton – Jean-Jacques Rousseau

Rousseau was one of the primary philosophers of the 18th century. His political writings had a profound influence on the French Revolution and although he was from Geneva (in what is now Switzerland), sixteen years after his death he was interred as a national hero of France in the Pantheon in Paris.

Raymond Cotton's play over the next few seasons at the quarterback position will have a profound influence on the success level of Ole Miss football. Although he is originally from Alabama and played his last year of high school football in Maryland, he will be a Mississippi hero should he lead the team to some big victories.

A.J. Hawkins – Martin Luther

Luther, the German monk and theologian, was the Father of Protestantism. By nailing his 95 theses to the door of the Castle Church in Wittenberg, he changed the course of the history of Western Civilization.

Hawkins, a 6'3" 315lb. center was a first-team 5A all-state performer in Georgia and was certainly one of the top 95 players in the state. He attended Martin Luther King High School in Lithonia.

Gabriel Hunter - Morgan Freeman

Although originally from Memphis; Freeman is one of Mississippi's favorite sons and makes his home in Charleston. José's generation knew him originally as "Easy Reader" on *The Electric Company*, but he is now identified as one of the great American actors and won the Academy Award for Best Supporting Actor for his role in *Million Dollar Baby*. He also played the role of God in *Bruce Almighty*.

Gabriel Hunter, a 5'11' running back, hails from Memphis and was named the 7th best player in Tennessee by the Knoxville News-Sentinel. Should Hunter someday contribute to a Rebel SEC football championship, he will be accorded divine-like status in Oxford.

Frank Crawford – Enrico Fermi

Enrico Fermi was one of the most important scientists of the 20th century. A physicist, known for his work on the Manhattan Project; he won the Nobel Prize for Physics in 1938 for his work on induced radioactivity. Although an extremely gifted scientist; in his day he was overshadowed by Einstein.

Crawford, the Miami, Florida native, was a PrepStar and SuperPrep All Region selection as a safety. Despite such accolades, he was somewhat overshadowed by his Gulliver Prep teammate and fellow Ole Miss signee, Artice Kellum.

Jamar Hornsby – Donnie Van Zandt

Van Zandt was the lead singer of the group .38 Special, which had hits such as "Hold on Loosely", "Caught Up in You" and "Second Chance". He hails from Jacksonville, Florida.

Jamar Hornsby, the #3 rated junior college player in the country by SuperPrep, is a Jacksonville, Florida native. The former Florida Gator safety looks to contribute immediately in the Rebel secondary after being given a second chance by Coach Houston Nutt.

Zaccheus Mason - Faisal bin Al Hussein Bin Ali El-Hashemi

Faisal, friend of T.E. Lawrence (Lawrence of Arabia) in his younger days, later became King of Syria and also King of Iraq. He sided with Great Britain in World War I, despite many of his Arab brothers accusing him of betraying Islam by fighting alongside Christians (translation: Presbyterians), and also assisted Allied forces in the capturing of Damascus.

Zaccheus Mason is not a wee little man. He is a 6'5" 255lb. tight end who caught 35 passes for 464 yards and also rushed for 489 yards as a senior. He was rated the #2 tight end prospect in the country and may very well prove to be the star of this class someday. He attended Christ Presbyterian Academy in Nashville and some Tennesseans felt betrayed when he picked the Rebels over the Volunteers.

Demarcus Knight – Pliny the Elder

Caius Plinius Secundus, or "Pliny the Elder", was an author, natural philosopher, and military commander in ancient Rome. His great work, *Naturalis Historia* (Natural History) was an encyclopedia that encompassed much of the knowledge of the day and included thirty-seven books. Pliny was a victim of the eruption of Mount Vesuvius in A.D. 79.

Demarcus Knight, a 6'2" 230 linebacker from Morristown, Tennessee was listed as the 37th rated middle-linebacker in the country by ESPN. He recorded 79 tackles his sophomore year. Due to the obvious similarities between him and Pliny the Elder, José strongly encourages Demarcus to steer clear of active volcanoes.

Charles Sawyer – Robert Urich

Urich was Dan Tanna on the television show *Vegas* and also starred in *Spencer: For Hire* as, you guessed it, Spencer. A native of Toronto, Ohio: Urich attended Florida State University on a football scholarship.

Sawyer, a 5'10" 180 lb. cornerback from Miami, Florida; turned down offers from the University of Florida and Michigan, among others, to sign with the Rebels. He hopes to appear on television in the BCS Championship game during his Ole Miss tenure.

Tyler Campbell – Arthur Conan Doyle

Famed author, Conan Doyle; the creator of the character Sherlock Holmes, was educated at a Roman Catholic Jesuit prep school. He practiced medicine for many years and served as a physician during the Boer War. Conan Doyle was knighted in 1902.

Tyler Campbell, a 6'2" punter from Little Rock attended Catholic High School. Considering Campbell comes to Ole Miss with a 3.5 GPA, a career in the medical field is not out of the question.

Michael Brown – Leon Leonwood Bean

Leon Leonwood better known as L.L., was an avid hunter and fisherman who created a mail-order catalog to sell the waterproof boots he created. His company went on to produce a full line of clothing and would have been profitable even if it only sold to Ole Miss students in the 1980's.

Michael Brown is a big ol' 6'6" 305lb. country boy from Lexington, Texas who likely hunts and fishes. He was born in 1991, which is around the time José decided it was time for a new pair of blucher moccasins.

Two parts down. One to go.

My name is José Valdez IV and these are my thoughts.

Notes:

- The "just a flesh wound" is another *Monty Python and the Holy Grail* reference.

- The "tennis twins bombed Pearl Harbor" comment is in reference to a poster on one of the message boards commenting that everyone should stop making the "Germans bomb Pearl Harbor" statements on the board in deference to the German twins on the Rebel tennis team. I just couldn't resist on that one.

- I recently read a biography of Alexander Hamilton and he is one of the most fascinating people in American history. I seriously contemplated naming my dog after him, but decided a one-syllable name would be better.

- Ulysses Everett McGill was the character portrayed by George Clooney in *O Brother Where Art Thou?*

- Jamar Hornsby was not given a third chance by Coach Nutt. Possibly because there is no corresponding .38 Special song for that.

My first pair of L.L. Bean Bluchers lasted many years and are still the most comfortable shoes I ever owned.

José's Thoughts on the 2009 Recruiting Class Part Tres

Once again, these are exceedingly long, so if you plan to read them all, you might consider taking a nap before (or during) doing so.

Well José has done it again. It seems that he always drives away the people he cares for the most.

José knows it is inevitable, yet he cannot prevent himself from doing things that make others uncomfortable. He has been given the nickname "Social Rainman" (which he does not dispute) for his inability to determine what is or is not appropriate in social situations. Unfortunately, much to his chagrin, the person José has now driven away is Coach Nutt.

It began innocently enough. José just wanted to thank Coach Nutt for the glorious football season and phenomenal recruiting class Nutt was responsible for. First he thought some kind of gift would be appropriate. But what to give Coach Nutt? Candlesticks always make a nice gift. Perhaps a place-setting or maybe a silverware pattern? No, José thought. A gift would not convey the genuine appreciation he had. He just needed to communicate his feelings verbally.

This was not necessarily a mistake in itself. The mistake was in not actually planning what to say before he saw Coach Nutt. José thought the words would just flow freely.

José arrived early yesterday morning and waited outside Coach Nutt's office, sombrero in hand. He eventually showed up.

"Coach Nutt?"

"Yes José?" (He still remembered José from the Wang Chung sing-along they shared after the Cotton Bowl. Things were going well at this point.)

"Coach Nutt. You… complete José."

Awkward.

Coach Nutt sprinted back to his vehicle; locked the doors and called security.

As things currently stand, the relationship between Coach Nutt and José could best be described as strained. José would appreciate it if any of you who consider yourself friends with the coach, could let him know that for the most part, José is harmless. Although on the surface there may appear to be many similarities between him and Steinbeck's Lennie Small, José has actually never harmed any person (or rabbit).

On to the task at hand. It is high time José concluded his thoughts on the 2009 recruiting class. Before he commits to composing thoughts again next year on the 2010 class he would like some assurance that there are no plans to sing 38 players. The extremely limited social life of José has been relegated to the occasional conversation with the person in the spot next to him on one of his late night Sonic runs.

Note: José is no expert on Keynesian Economics, but it seems to him that bringing back the $.99 root beer float could have nothing but positive effect on the economy.

Due to numerous people stating that the comparisons José used in his prior two offerings were blatantly obvious and almost exactly similar to their own, he has chosen not to go with the first person who came to mind when thinking of a particular recruit, but instead offers the fifth person he thought of. Hopefully this list is either different than yours or you only went four deep.

The thirteen remaining recruits:

Willie Ferrell – Woodrow Wilson

Ferrell, from Florida A&M High School, was the #6 rated inside linebacker in the country according to ESPN. He was also a two-time member of the Tallahassee Democrat All-Big Bend team.

Woodrow "Willie" Wilson, a Democrat, was rated the 6th best president of all-time in a 1999 C-Span poll.

Logan Clair – Geronimo

Clair is a 6'5" 310lb. juco transfer offensive lineman. He should provide immediate depth on the Rebel O-line if he tramples defenders like he has been known to do. He lettered three years at Mustang High School in Mustang, Oklahoma.

Geronimo spent a few of his years in Oklahoma and rode a Mustang while trampling a few pale faces.

Craig Drummond – Conrad Bain

Drummond is an Army All-American defensive end from Chicago, Illinois that the Rebels jumped on late in the recruiting process and who could be a tremendous difference-maker.

Bain played Mr. Drummond on *Different Strokes.*

Emmanuel McCray- James Watt

McCray, the 6'4" 280 lb. star from Forest Hill High School in Jackson, was the #22 rated prospect in Mississippi according to SuperPrep.

Watt developed the steam engine and was named the 22nd most influential person in history in a book by Michael Hart.

Jessie Grandy – Cai Lun

Grandy, the 4A Arkansas defensive player of the year, had eight interceptions while leading Dollarway High School team to the state championship game his senior season. He was the subject of numerous newspaper articles in his local paper.

Cai Lun served under Emperor He during the Han Dynasty. He is generally credited with being the inventor of paper. Had he invented edible paper the world would not have the garbage problem it currently faces.

Dele Junaid – Ty Murray

Junaid, a 6'3" 195 lb. defensive back from Hightower High School in Sugarland, was a second-team all 5A pick in Texas his senior season.

Murray, the rodeo champion, resides in Stephenville, Texas (home of Jaylon and Jevan Snead) with his wife, recording star Jewel. They are currently competing against one another on *Dancing With the Stars* (so José is told). Murray's dance partner is Cherie Hightower.

Montez Phillips – Napoleon Bonaparte

The Corsican Bonaparte, became a military and political leader of France, shaping much of 19th century European politics in the process. He also freed The Marquis de Lafayette from an Austrian prison in 1797.

Alex Williams – Robert Duvall

Williams, a 6'4" 215 lb. defensive end from Tallahassee, was named to the Florida first team All-State squad in both his junior and senior seasons. His brother, Boo, played for Houston Nutt at Arkansas.

In his first movie role, Duvall played the character Boo Radley in *To Kill a Mockingbird.*

Rodney Scott – Daniel Emmett

Scott, the much-heralded Florida running back, rushed for over 3,600 yards and scored 51 touchdowns during his junior and senior seasons at Dixie County High School.

Daniel Emmett (a Yankee) wrote the song "Dixie".

Stephen Houston – Billy Mills

Houston, a 5"10 190 lb. athlete from Lakota West High School in West Chester, Ohio, was rated the 103rd best running back by Scout.com.

Mills won the gold medal in the 10,000 meter run at the 1964 Tokyo Olympics in what is considered one of the great upsets in Olympic history. Mills is a member of the Oglala Lakota (Sioux) Tribe. Robbie Benson played Mills in a movie, but it was not the one that involved the red-hot poker.

Ryan Campbell – Byron Stewart

Campbell, a 6'0" 170 lb. defensive back from Columbus, Georgia, earned 1ˢᵗ team Class 3A All-State honors from the Associated Press while leading Carver High School to the state semi-finals his senior season.

Stewart played "Coolidge" on *The White Shadow*. Coolidge led his Carver High School team to the Los Angeles City Championship in 1980.

Joel Kight – Khaled Hosseini

Kight, a 5'11" (so they say) 220lb. linebacker from Lithonia, was named Georgia 5A first-team All-State in both his junior and senior seasons. ESPN rated him the 47ᵗʰ best outside linebacker in the country.

Hosseini wrote the Kite Runner.

Mike Thomas – Mike Thomas

Thomas, a 6'4" 245 lb. defensive lineman from St. Paul's Episcopal School in Mobile, Alabama, was rated the 24ᵗʰ best player in Alabama by SuperPrep.

José really struggled with this one. There weren't five people he could come up with who came to mind when he thought about Mike Thomas. He could have taken the Episcopal affiliation and gone with Batman, since many people believe Batman is Episcopalian. But José could not in good conscience use a comic book hero, no matter how awesome he is. So he just googled "Mike Thomas" and discovered that there is a realtor who apparently sells more listings in Northeast Indiana than anyone else, named Mike Thomas. Not too shabby.

My name is José Valdez IV and these are my thoughts.

Notes:
- **When I began the thoughts on the recruiting class a few weeks prior with part one, I had no idea how difficult it would be. The first part was fine. The second one was a little more challenging. I was sick of them by the time I wrote the third part. I doubt I'll ever attempt to do these again.**

Fortunately for me, the SEC changed the rule and you may no longer sign that many players.

- The part about trying to decide what kind of gift to give Coach Nutt is from the classic visit to the mound scene in *Bull Durham*.

- "You complete me" is of course from *Jerry McGuire*.

- Lennie Small is a character in Steinbeck's *Of Mice and Men*.

- The "edible paper" reference comes from the movie *Night Shift*.

- I made a mistake in these thoughts and forgot to write about the connection Montez Phillips had to Bonaparte. A few people caught this and recognized that I had mentioned the Marquis de Lafayette and that Phillips had attended Lafayette High School. The latest word on Phillips is that he may opt for a baseball career so maybe my neglecting to write about him may have been prophetic.

José's Thoughts on the 12th Opponent

The selection of a 12th football opponent for the Ole Miss 2009 football season has been the source of much consternation among the Rebel faithful. It is imperative that at least a decent BCS (or Division 1 if you still prefer to call it that) team be selected as the opponent since this has a chance to be a special team and computer rankings could come into play as to where the Rebels play their final game. José has heard it said that should the Rebels go unbeaten (and he can't believe it has come to the point where people are even contemplating that possibility) then there is no way they could be kept out of the BCS Championship game. He does not argue that. However, a one-loss team, that ends up winning the SEC Championship could lose out on such an opportunity if it played two 1-AA (or whatever the hell they're called now) opponents during the season. That possibility frightens José.

Selfishly though, the selection of a 12th opponent is a matter of great importance to José as he must share his thoughts on whomever the opponent proves to be, so for his sake, the more interesting the better.

With this in mind, José offers his comments on some potential opponents and why they would or would not make good choices.

University of Pittsburgh – Home of the tallest educational building in the Western Hemisphere. Boring.

University of Arizona- They feature what José believes to be the only "married" mascots, Wilbur and Wilma Wildcat. Also, the school's grading system does not include "F"'s, only "E"'s, for fear of harming someone's self-esteem. José can work with that.

University of California- Santa Cruz – Their nickname is the Banana Slugs. Unfortunately they don't field a football team.

University of Michigan- Playing the Wolverines would give José an opportunity to describe his experience at the 1991 Gator Bowl (which other than the actual game was spectacular). JFK proposed The Peace Corps on the steps of the Michigan Union in 1960. José has had more success with Peace Corps chicks than any other demographic (including Indigo Girl groupies).

University of Houston- Not much going for Houston other than the fact that the character of "Van" on the television show *Reba* received a football scholarship offer from U of H. God help you if you were already aware of that.

University of Kansas- Bob Dole is from Kansas. He has been known to speak in third person, which is odd. They also boast of a student organization called "Drinking Conservatively" which apparently involves getting liquored up on Thursday nights while discussing the merits of trickle-down economic policies and whatnot.

University of Utah- Utah is the home of the best-known chapter of the "Flying Elvises". They have a fierce rivalry with Brigham Young University, which means that the people of each school do not speak to each other on game day.

Indiana University- Sportscaster Joe Buck is an alumnus of the school. José is not a fan.

Central Michigan University- The Chippewas were placed on a list of "hostile and abusive" nicknames by the NCAA in 2005 to which the nearby Saginaw Chippewa Indian Tribe responded "up yours NCAA" and CMU was able to keep its nickname. Plus the dude who plays John Locke on *Lost* went to school there.

Florida State University- FSU claims they invented streaking, when in 1974, 200 students ran naked across campus one March evening. Since he was not there, José cannot state it as fact, but he surmises that this group of

200 probably included 180 guys and 20 plus-sized chicks. Mass streaking groups are typically composed of such.

Wait. What is that you are saying to José? The 12th opponent was announced last week and it is the University of Northern Arizona Lumberjacks?
Well that pretty much sucks.

My name is José Valdez IV and these are my thoughts.

Notes:

- **It was frightening to even write about the possibility of Ole Miss playing in the BCS championship game and time will tell if it was a pipedream.**

- **My 1991 Gator Bowl experience was not that exciting. The game was probably the highlight and the Rebels lost 35-3.**

- **The "Flying Elvises" reference is from *Honeymoon in Vegas*.**

- **All of the items listed for the different schools are factual.**

José's thoughts on The School Whose Name Shall Not be Spoken Chapter Cuatro

Please forgive José for the failure to share his thoughts on a regular basis in recent days. He would like to blame it on general laziness, which is typically the case when he does nothing of any redeeming social value for a significant period of time. The simple fact is that he has been recuperating from a slight injury he sustained while trying to reenact Van Halen's "Panama" video for a YouTube production that Jorge, Paco and he had in the works. That project has since been scrapped in favor of a dramatic retelling of the story of the Donner Party, from the perspective of the first guy that was eaten.

Tonight's Governor's Trophy game against The School Whose Name Shall not be Spoken (TSWNSNBS) offers José an opportunity to share his thoughts on one of his favorite subjects. There are probably some people who are thinking "Wasn't this game formerly called the Mayor's Trophy?" That is correct and José is not sure exactly why the name was changed but he believes it has something to do with the fact that the Mayor of Jackson started tearing down houses with his bare hands and comporting himself in a manner indistinguishable from Daniel Plainview in *There Will be Blood*.

Regarding TSWNSNBS, it has come to the point that José almost feels sorry for them. They have the 10th best baseball team in the Southeastern Conference (possibly 11th, pending the outcome of this weekend's games); the one sport in which they have had at least some reason to boast historically. Their football team is set to continue its tradition of ineptitude in 2009. When the new coach is not busy searching for a cowbell app for his iPhone, he is preparing the masses for how bad things should be, months in advance of the season opener. A player was quoted after one of the early spring practices as saying, "It wasn't a complete waste of time." José begs to differ. It was a complete waste of time. Most of their players would be better served by joining the nearest "Up with People" troupe than attempting to line up against SEC opponents for the next few years. It is not going to be pretty. But this is really nothing new for their fans. TSWNSNBS has participated in thirteen bowl games in their 120+ year history of playing football. To put this in perspective, José has been forcibly removed from Christmas cantata's on more occasions than that.

But José digresses. Tonight is about baseball. Of course this is a meaningless game as far as conference play goes, but if your team is 5-10 in league play and has been surpassed by your rival as the dominant in-state program, then you are probably working yourself into a lather right about now. Chances are, that should TSWNSNBS somehow manage a victory, you'll see maroon "2009 Governor's Cup Champs" t-shirts on sale in West Point by Thursday. The truly sad part is those shirts will likely still be worn in 2025 (to both weddings and job interviews).

John Cohen, the new baseball coach at TSWNSNBS, is obnoxious. Make no mistake, he despises Ole Miss, so should you happen to find yourself within earshot of Cohen at Trustmark Park tonight, please heckle the man on José's behalf. You might inquire as to how it feels to have a direct hand in two of the three worst baseball teams in the conference. Or just ask if Ron Polk has accepted his Facebook friend request.

My name is José Valdez IV and these are my thoughts.

Notes:

- **In case you aren't familiar with the "Panama" video, the members of Van Halen fly over the stage harnessed to some kind of wire apparatus. It looked like fun to me.**

- **The Donner party was a group of people that were attempting to relocate to California in the 1840's. They became stranded in the Sierra Nevada's and resorted to cannibalism.**

- **When I wrote the comment about the coach searching for a cowbell app for his iPhone I honestly had no idea that one actually existed.**

José's Thoughts on Double Decker Weekend

José had two choices of things to do this past weekend. He could go to Oxford for Double Decker and the Rebel baseball series against Georgia, or he could sit around the house. Had he chosen the latter he likely would have spent way too much time on Facebook, sending friend requests to miscellaneous ladies in the Magee, Mississippi vicinity (there are some crazy ones there from what he hears) and working his way through various pick five lists until he got to "Top Five Legumes" (which would be peanuts, purple hull peas, black eyed peas, snap beans and butter beans in case you are interested). Fortunately José chose the former option.

José did not attend the Friday night baseball game so he cannot be held responsible for the outcome that evening. Had he been there he would have been the one yelling profanities in Spanish while being removed from the ballpark by security after the Georgia grand slam. Thanks to his portable radio, he was instead removed from little Josélina's piano recital. Do not concern yourself over Josélina being embarrassed by her father's behavior though as she isn't fazed by much since the video of José at Bid Day 1984 first surfaced on the internet.

Her: "So Dad, you mean to tell me there was a time when it was cool for a guy to wear a bandana?"

José: "Actually no, sugar. There wasn't."

Saturday was open though after José completed a couple of hours of charity work (sometimes referred to as court-appointed community service) so he, Jorge and Paco headed to Oxford for Double Decker and baseball. It would be a long and tedious process to relate the entire story of what occurred on Saturday and Sunday so instead, José offers a few observations.

- "My name is José Valdez IV" does not work as a pick-up line. Neither does "So, do you need a drink or a place to stay?" On the other hand, you'd be surprised with how effective "I owned The Gin" can be with the recently divorced 40+ crowd.

- Being trapped in a Port-o-John for four hours does not have to be a complete waste of your time. If you're close enough to one of the stages you can still hear the band and the acoustics aren't that bad. You may also use the time to brush up on your memorization of the state capitals (New Jersey's is Trenton and Washington's is Olympia. Those two tend to trip people up).

- Apparently it is not the practice of the Presbyterian church in Oxford to stand up before the congregation and publicly confess your sins of the prior evening. However if you must, you should probably wait until after they dismiss for children's church.

- The atmosphere at the baseball games was incredible. The NCAA should take note and make the Rebels permanent regional and super regional hosts no matter what their record is.

- This baseball team is gritty. They are not the most talented Rebel team of recent years (at least not offensively), but they are about as mentally tough as any group seen here in a long time. The team with Head, Pettway, Coghlan and Cozart was an extremely tough group that unfortunately lost an excruciating Super Regional to the eventual national champions, but José will put this bunch in the same class in the intestinal fortitude department. It remains to be seen whether this will be the team that finally gets to Omaha. You can be certain though that they will battle until the final out every time they step on the field.

All in all it was a great weekend to be in Oxford (but isn't every weekend)? The music was great, the women were gorgeous, and the tequila was readily accessible. Also, José happened to notice that the house he lived in his final year in school is now for sale. He is currently seeking investment partners who are willing to provide 125% of the capital (needs some walking around money also) in order to secure this property.

Finally, José must digress momentarily to address the criticism he has received over his obvious bias towards Presbyterians and against the Baptists. Some have inferred from prior thoughts that he does not believe Baptists can go to heaven. He would like to state for the record that he is quite certain that Baptists can go to heaven, provided they don't chew gum in church.

My name is José Valdez IV and these are my thoughts.

Notes:

- **There really are some crazy stories about certain events that have transpired in Magee.**

- **There is no video of me at Bid Day 1984 to my knowledge and I did not wear a bandana.**

- **I did try the "So do you need a drink or a place to stay?" on a few occasions many years ago. As with my other pick-up lines, it was unsuccessful.**

- **My two boys enjoy being quizzed about the state capitals.**

- **I did visit Christ Presbyterian in Oxford that Sunday, but made no such confessions.**

- **Brian Pettway now coaches a 12 year-old baseball team in the Jackson area and my son Wes plays against him on occasion.**

- **The house I once lived in, on 11th Avenue, was for sale when I went by, and I would love to live there.**

José's Thoughts on The School Whose Name Shall Not be Spoken Chapter Cinco

The School Whose Name Shall Not be Spoken is perilously close to losing "Shall Not be Spoken" status with José. To be considered among the pantheon of things of which José will not speak of, one must at least maintain some semblance of relevance. TSWNSNBS is no longer relevant in football or baseball. Basketball is really the only thing left going for it, and that could soon change if it is discovered that their recent recruits are opening off-shore bank accounts and offering to assist with the GM bailout.

Of course losing SNBS status with José is not unprecedented. There have been some recent changes, for various reasons, which are listed below.

- The Coach Whose Name Shall Not be Spoken- Tommy Tuberville. The Rebels whipped him in their final meeting and he's no longer employed as a coach. Should he return to the coaching ranks and someday defeat Ole Miss, he has the possibility of regaining his status. For now, he's just Tommy Tuberville, the jerk.

- The Prom Date Whose Name Shall Not be Spoken- Consuela Sanchez. She sent José a Facebook friend request and suggested they relive some pre-prom memories, so they are good now.

- The Human Resources Director Whose Name Shall Not be Spoken- Scott McDonald. The whole misunderstanding about which Salma Hayek screensavers are "workplace appropriate" has been resolved.

- The Career Counselor Whose Name Shall Not be Spoken- Candace Fleming. She recently had some "augmentation" work done (very successful might José add) and it just seems silly to hold a grudge at this point over her suggestion that José's aspirations of being a naked sage of India were unreasonable and that he was probably best suited to be a carnie.

- The 8th Grade Algebra Teacher Whose Name Shall Not be Spoken- Mrs. Woods. She's dead now. Mrs. Woods is no more. She has rung down the curtain and joined the choir invisible. She is an ex-algebra teacher.

But José digresses.

Despite their obvious irrelevance in baseball, José will maintain his TSWNSNBS stance for these thoughts. Times are indeed tough for them. A generation of their fans is now seeing many of their children abandon ship, and truthfully, who can blame them? What self-respecting 12 year-old boy would choose to go to Starkville for a weekend to see the dregs of the Southeastern Conference when his friends invite him to go to Oxford and enjoy a weekend of Rebel baseball at the finest facility in the country? Add the possibility of Big Bad Breakfast and it's a no-brainer. Some parents have completely thrown in the towel on the likelihood of their children attending TSWNSNBS, and have focused their efforts on encouraging them to go out of state. Unfortunately for them, the appeal of Ole Miss will be too strong for some of these kids and they are more than willing to work in the summer in order to purchase some non maroon-colored articles of clothing. In fact, the following occurs about fifteen times daily.

"Dad, you do realize that other than that Saturday Night Live sketch, cowbells are about the uncoolest things out there? Please don't make me take one out in public."

As for the actual series this weekend, José has no hesitancy in predicting a Rebel victory. The only question is whether or not it will be a sweep. With much still on the line for this Ole Miss team, you can expect that they will give their typical effort, which is relentless. You can also expect that Ron Polk will be turning over in his grave this weekend.

Wait. Ron Polk isn't dead? What about Jack Cristil? Not dead either? Bet they sometimes wish they were.

My name is José Valdez IV and these are my thoughts.

Notes:

- **The Rebels lost two of three in this series, which was terrible. I like to think the blame lies less with me than with the fact that we bunted after a leadoff double in the 4th inning of the first game with the score tied 2-2.**

- **My 8th grade algebra teacher was actually a man. He hated me. I am unaware of whether or not he has joined the choir invisible, which is a reference from the classic Monty Python "Dead Parrot" sketch.**

- **I had just made my maiden voyage to Big Bad Breakfast the week before writing these thoughts. It was unbelievable. Marty Stuart was there enjoying himself as well.**

José's Thoughts on the SEC Championship

1977.

"What is significant about 1977 José?" you ask.

Well there are many things. For example:

- The television mini-series "Roots" takes the nation by storm.

- José attends his first Ole Miss football game.

- Roy Sullivan, a park ranger in Virginia, is struck by lightning for the seventh time.

- José is given a lifetime ban from attending Vacation Bible School at First Baptist Jackson for his repeated questioning of the Noah's Ark story.

- Elvis dies.

- The Ole Miss Rebels win the regular season Southeastern Conference Championship in baseball, their last such championship in any of the big three sports until now.

As he has previously stated, there have been many times over the years that José has cursed José III for saddling him with the burden of being an Ole Miss fan. If one is honest, it has not been a particularly rewarding experience for those of José's generation. But there were signs that things might be changing this past football season. Still, who would have expected that an Ole Miss team going into Arkansas without their best pitcher and trailing LSU by a game, would come away with an SEC title? In years past, a team that had just lost two of three at home to TSWNSNBS would have gone into Arkansas and been swept, or won one game at most. But this team responded with a sweep and the championship. It is particularly gratifying that the Rebels won it in Arkansas, the state where Maya Angelou spent her formative years.

Since Saturday, numerous people have approached José and inquired as to how he celebrated the Rebels title clinching victory. *Note: Actually no one has asked José about this, but for the purposes of these thoughts, go with him on it.*

Let's just say that his celebration was much different than the one in 1977 when he offered Carmelita Benitez an ice-cold IBC root beer and attempted to make out with her. The combination of an SEC championship and the root beer was apparently not enough to overcome the terry cloth shirt, red gym shorts and tube socks that were José's standard attire that summer. *Note: José recently ran into Carmelita and she has unpardonably thick ankles these days.*

The 2009 celebration involved tequila, cigars, Listerine (to get rid of the cigar taste), a game of strip poker (via WebEx), and a late night drive to Yazoo City. The trip was in order to relive the night that Jorge, Paco and José, after discovering where she was staying for the filming of *Miss Firecracker*, stood on the sidewalk outside and yelled lines from *Raising Arizona* to Holly Hunter (primarily "Turn to the right!" and "You go up there and get me a baby!") until she came outside and began shouting profanities at them. *Note: The present occupant of the home is apparently unfamiliar with Raising Arizona, was not amused either, and unlike Miss Hunter, is proficient with a crossbow. But seldom is the night when one of the three of them comes away without some sort of flesh wound, so they were none the worse for the wear and all in all, it was a glorious evening.*

Now the focus for the Rebels moves to getting to Omaha. Two or three wins in the SEC Tournament may be what is needed in order to get a national seed. Finishing better than Florida is probably what is most important though. So for those of you headed to Birmingham, a few "31-30" or "Tebow wears Greg Hardy pajamas" chants would be welcome. The trash-talking José V may be in attendance. He repeatedly yelled "Who's your dealer?" to Gary Sheffield at a spring training game after steroid revelations appeared and will have no hesitancy in joining in any such fun at the tournament.

It is an exciting time to be a Rebel and allowed to cross state lines.

My name is José Valdez IV and these are my thoughts.

Notes:

- My first Ole Miss football game was the 1977 season-opening 7-3 win over Memphis State. This was also the year they beat Notre Dame, which I attended as well.

- I established my dislike for Maya Angelou in previous thoughts.

- My 1977 attire described in these thoughts is fairly accurate.

- I honestly do know a Carmelita Benitez. I went to high school with her and she was a great girl. The name just seemed to work perfectly for some of the thoughts.

- The Holly Hunter story is a true story, but I wasn't involved. It actually happened to my friend Keith Ball, and his friend Clark Spencer. According to Keith, she didn't really curse at them, but instead came out and said, "This is not cool guys. This is NOT cool." I still laugh picturing it.

- My older son Will was the one who yelled "Who's your dealer?" to Gary Sheffield. He also yelled "You stink!" to Mel Stottlemyre, the 70-something year-old pitching coach of the Yankees. He really doesn't like the Yankees in case you were wondering.

José's Thoughts on Virginia

Before sharing his thoughts on Virginia, José must address the performance by Drew Pomeranz that propelled the Rebels into this weekend's Super Regional. José has been present at some amazing pitching performances in his day. He witnessed Jack Morris throw ten shutout innings in the seventh game of the 1991 World Series. He also saw Pedro Martinez take a no-hitter into the 9th inning against the Tampa Bay Devil Rays in a game that featured a bench clearing brawl. Neither of those was as impressive as what Pomeranz did on Monday night. Sadly, José was not present at the game against Western Kentucky Monday night due to an unfortunate incident that necessitated he be quarantined for a brief period. He did however, watch every pitch on his computer and he's never seen anything better. Had Pomeranz just thrown your average run-of-the mill two-hitter it would have been special. Consider all of the pressure that he carried on his shoulders after the collapse of the previous day, and it is the stuff of legend. Throw in the fact that he did it on two days rest and it becomes transcendent. Here's hoping that you do, but chances are you will never see a more clutch individual performance by a Rebel in your lifetime.

But José digresses. On to Virginia.

The team standing in the way of the Rebels advancing to Omaha is the University of Virginia. There are many similarities between Ole Miss and Virginia. José has visited many college campuses for reasons which should not concern you, and although quite a few are very nice, in his estimation two stand out; Ole Miss and the University of Virginia. Ole Miss has the Grove. Virginia, the Lawn. Ole Miss has the Lyceum. Virginia, the Rotunda. Most are aware that John Grisham owns homes in both Oxford and Charlottesville. Also, UVA is home to many secret societies including the "Seven Society", "Eli Banana", and the "Purple Shadows". Ole Miss has the "47 Club" and many other societies so secret that José is unaware of their existence.

You may also be interested to know that the University of Virginia has an endowment of approximately $3.9 billion, which works out to about $191,000 per student; a figure that would pay off all seven of José's mortgages, the gambling debt he incurred for betting on *Saving Private Ryan* to win the 71st Academy Award for Best Picture (freakin *Shakespeare in Love*. Give me a break), and his bar tab at Raiford's Hollywood Disco with enough left over to buy a few 40's there.

"So you have told us many good things about Virginia, José" you say. "But I need something that will rile my passion against them for this weekend."

Point taken. It is important to feel some sort of animosity toward your opponent. José offers the following to help you in this regard.

Tiki Barber went to Virginia. The selfish one who was critical of Ole Miss legend Eli Manning, only to see Archie's boy lead his team to a Super Bowl Championship the year after he retired.

"That's okay" you say. "But I'm not sure it gives me the motivation I need to really let UVA have it this weekend."

José understands. Well how about this? Virginia killed William Faulkner.

For those who were not aware. Faulkner served as Writer in Residence at the University of Virginia from 1957 until they killed him in 1962.

"That is an outlandish accusation José" you say. "Faulkner died of a heart attack in Byhalia, Mississippi.

Look, all José knows is that Faulkner was in pretty good health when he went off to Virginia and when he returned to Mississippi he was dead within a few months. You can believe what you want to believe but José knows the deal.

Killing Faulkner or not, the time has come to take the next step and advance to Omaha. Rebel teams have been so close over the past few years and many Ole Miss fans are not old enough to remember the last time they played in a College World Series. So you must be prepared to be in Oxford this weekend and cheer like you have never done so before. There can be no let downs. When things are going well you need to be raucous. Don't let the Cavaliers ever think they have a chance. Conversely, if there comes a time when things look bleak, you need to pick the team up. Never let it be said that you did not give your all when the Rebels needed you most.

Another thing you can do is pray. Now José is not one who normally condones bartering with God, and is not sure about His interest in college baseball, but in this instance he is making an exception. He is fully prepared to remove the objectionable picture from his Facebook page, publicly apologize for the disturbance he caused at José V's baptism, and cancel his subscription to Match.com if God will just allow this Ole Miss team to make it to the College World Series. José suggests you consider what you are willing to sacrifice as well.

It's time. Yes, it is time for the Rebels to overcome their El Guapo. Everyone has an El Guapo to face someday. For some, shyness might be their El Guapo. For others, a lack of education might be their El Guapo. For the people of Santa Poco, El Guapo is a big dangerous guy who wants to kill them and who also happens to be the actual El Guapo. For the Ole Miss baseball team, the Super Regionals have been their El Guapo. But as sure as my name is José Valdez IV, this particular Rebel baseball team can conquer their own personal El Guapo who comes this weekend in the form of the University of Virginia.

Your job as a fan is to step up this weekend the way Drew Pomeranz stepped up Monday night. José will be there and will be loud. Hopefully his "UVA killed Faulkner" sign will get some airtime on ESPN 2.

My name is José Valdez IV and these are my thoughts.

Notes:

- **I mentioned in a previous offering that I was present for games six and seven of the 1991 World Series.**

- **I was not able to attend the Western Kentucky game but watched every pitch on my computer in a hotel room in Mason, Ohio.**

- **A great response to these thoughts on the José Facebook page came from Margaret Weems Feldmayer, who wrote "You had me at Tiki."**

- **I used "El Guapo" from *The Three Amigos* in prior thoughts but had never quoted the great speech from Steve Martin about everyone having to face their own El Guapo.**

- **Every Rebel fans knows that once again, Ole Miss won the first game, yet ended up losing the Super Regional. I was able to refrain from writing my thoughts about why that happened.**

Acknowledgements

I am very grateful to my family, Janna, Will, Wes and Reagan, for their patience and understanding as I spent many nights working on this project.

My father, Jim Crockett (the real author in the family) and brother Craig have both been very encouraging.

I have a few friends who knew I was the person writing these thoughts and they have been extremely supportive throughout. They include Sam Hubbard, William Foushee, Bob Mims, Jody Varner and Keith Ball. I also appreciate their keeping my identity secret these many months.

Chuck Rounsaville at the Ole Miss Spirit and Neal McCready at RebelSports.net could not have been more gracious and helpful to me. For that I am very appreciative.

Finally, I owe my biggest debt of gratitude to the readers and posters on the Ole Miss Spirit and RebelSports.net message boards. Their responses encouraged me and made the entire process worth while.